D0178802

CHRISTMAS CROSS STITCH

Christmas Cross Stitch

OVER 50 TRADITIONAL DESIGNS

CHRIS TIMMS

HAMLYN

To my husband, Gareth, as he is so fond of Christmas

CHRISTMAS CROSS STITCH
Chris Timms

First published in Great Britain in 1994
by Hamlyn
an imprint of Reed Consumer Books Limited
Michelin House, 81 Fulham Road London SW3 6RB
and Auckland, Melbourne, Singapore and Toronto

First paperback edition 1995

Art Editor LISA TAI
Editors CATHERINE WARD AND PATSY NORTH
Executive Editor JUDITH MORE
Art Director JACQUI SMALL
Photography MARK WILLIAMS
Title Page Picture SIMON BROWN
Styling SIRI HILLS
Production ALISON MYER

A CIP record for this book is available from the British Library

ISBN 0 600 58747 9

The publishers have made very effort to ensure that all instructions given in this book are accurate and safe, but they cannot accept liability for any resulting injury, damage or loss to either person or property whether direct or consequential and howsoever arising. The author and publishers will be grateful for any information which will assist them in keeping future editions up to date.

Typeset in Caslon 540 Roman, Caslon 3, Kuenstler Script Medium and Cochin
Index compiled by Leigh Priest
Colour origination by Alphabet Set
Produced by Mandarin Offset
Printed and bound in Hong Kong

Contents

Foreword

When I first started thinking about this book, I had visions of candlelight and firelight on burnished gold decorations, fir trees covered with candles, nuts and gilded pine cones, boughs of holly, festive wreaths and large bunches of mistletoe. In fact, all the trappings of an old-fashioned Christmas in the best tradition. The items I have designed for *Christmas Cross Stitch* reflect this idea.

The first chapter features a selection of embroidered cards, which will look pretty displayed on any mantlepiece. Also included are a variety of gift tags, which will add a personal touch to your parcels with their simple but effective motifs.

The pictures in the second chapter are much larger and, consequently, more time-consuming to stitch, but they are of seasonal designs which will look charming in your house all year round. They all have children as their theme, and are delightful cameos of the exciting events of Christmas.

The next chapter contains not only some unusual decorations to hang on your tree, but also two mantlepiece borders which will transform your fireplace. The decorations include embroidered baubles, and miniature stockings and sacks which you can fill with sweets before hanging on the tree.

The fourth chapter will solve all your Christmas shopping problems as it contains a wealth of gifts which I hope will please everyone, from a glasses case and a brooch pin to a large, embroidered cushion.

The three festive table settings in the next chapter feature tartan, mistletoe and geese motifs. I have included a tablecloth, napkins, napkin rings, tablemats and doilies which you can bring out year after year. There is even a mistletoe-carrying rabbit on a bib to make for baby, so she can join in the festivities. In fact, everything you need to make your Christmas special, apart from the food and drink.

A Happy Christmas to one and all!

Christmas Cards

A home-made card, especially a stitched one, is so much nicer to receive than a bought one. The recipient feels that the giver must really care, to have gone to so much trouble. The cards that my own children and grandchildren have given me over the years are much treasured; I have stored them all away carefully and take them out sentimentally now and again to have a nostalgic look through them. The cards and gift tags in this chapter will not only look lovely standing on a mantelpiece or displayed on a wall at Christmas, but can also be framed as little pictures and hung up in your home. A child, particularly, would like to have pictures like these in his or her room.

The cardboard mounts for your pictures can be customized or personalized in many ways. You can sponge them randomly with gold or silver paint, perhaps achieving a rich finish by using two different shades of gold. Another method of applying colour and texture is to screw up a piece of paper, dip it into your saucer of paint and dab it over the cardboard. Experiment first on a spare piece of scrap paper or cardboard until you achieve the desired effect. If you drag a paintbrush with two different shades of gold, or gold and then bronze or copper, across the card in opposite directions, you will get a subtle but smart striped effect. Or you could dip a stiff brush such as a stencil brush into a small amount of paint (be careful to mop up any excess paint on the

brush on a piece of absorbent kitchen paper) and – again, having practised first on some scrap paper or cardboard – flick the brush to make tiny speckles of colour on your chosen cardboard. Spattered white paint looks good on dark cardboard such as a deep blue. As an alternative to spattering, you could hold the stencil brush vertically and dab it onto the cardboard to create an uneven smattering of colour.

Another original way of decorating a cardboard mount is to stencil or spray it with gold or silver paint through a paper doily or some old lace. Then you can cut gold paper or foil into a zigzag pattern and stick it around the outside of the card. The gold- or silver-sprayed doily or lace can itself be stuck onto the card too. Tartan ribbon can look highly effective, either glued on flat as a border or tied into bows and stuck onto each corner of the card.

The snowdrops gift tag, and indeed any of the other small designs featured in this chapter, can also be used as greetings cards if you don't have time to make a more intricate design. You could make them up with a larger, framed edging and decorate that, so that the cards will still have that special personal touch without having taken too long to create.

On the other hand, if you decide to use the smaller designs as gift tags, it would be a nice idea to co-ordinate your gift by decorating your wrapping paper to match. Plain brown or lining paper can look unexpectedly sophisticated if you give it an edging that echoes the design of the gift tag.

Girl with Toys

This finely worked card shows a gleeful girl running through the snow carrying her new toys. With such delicate stitching, you can show tiny details and subtle shading.

Measurements

The actual design measures 6 x 9.75cm (2⅜ x 3¾in)

Materials

• Piece of white 22-count Hardanger fabric measuring 16 x 19.75cm (6¼ x 7¾in)
• DMC or Anchor stranded embroidery cotton, one skein each of the colours shown in the chart
• Tapestry needle, size 26
• Red cardboard mount with rectangular aperture measuring 9 x 11.5cm (3½ x 4½in)
• Firm brown paper

To make up

Following the chart and beginning centrally (see p.104), work the design in cross stitch using one strand of embroidery thread. Each square represents one cross stitch. Where squares are shown divided diagonally, with half in one colour and half in another colour, work three-quarter cross stitches (see p.105). When all the cross stitching is complete, add the features in back stitch and satin stitch using one strand of embroidery thread in the colours shown on the chart.

Press the completed work on the reverse using a hot iron setting (see p.106), then make up the card following the instructions given on p.106. For a decorative mount, cut a piece of firm brown paper to show just inside the aperture of the card.

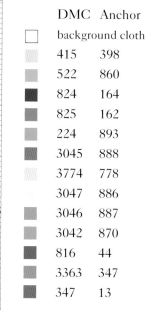

DMC	Anchor
	background cloth
415	398
522	860
824	164
825	162
224	893
3045	888
3774	778
3047	886
3046	887
3042	870
816	44
3363	347
347	13

Downhill Run

This design shows two rosy-cheeked children skimming through the snow on their sledge with the wind in their hair. It would make an extra-special card for a youngster in your family.

Measurements

The actual design measures 6.5 x 7.5cm (2½ x 3in)

Materials

• Piece of off-white 16-count aida fabric measuring 21 x 22cm (8¼ x 8½in)
• DMC or Anchor stranded embroidery cotton, one skein each of the colours shown in the chart
• Tapestry needle, size 26
• Dark-blue cardboard mount with rectangular aperture measuring 9.5 x 7.5cm (3¾ x 3in)
• Gold pen

To make up

Following the chart and beginning centrally (see p.104), work the design in cross stitch using two strands of embroidery thread. Each square represents one cross stitch. When all the cross stitching is complete, add the children's features in back stitch and straight stitch using one strand of embroidery thread in the colours shown in the chart. With two strands of brown thread, make a rope for the sledge by looping it through the boy's hands as shown in the chart.

Press the completed work on the reverse using a hot iron setting (see p.106), then make up the card following the instructions given on p.106. As an extra decorative touch, add a border around the aperture using a gold pen and a ruler.

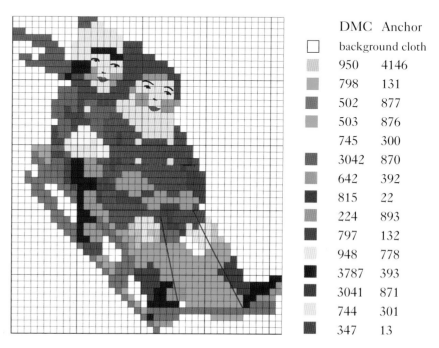

	DMC	Anchor
		background cloth
	950	4146
	798	131
	502	877
	503	876
	745	300
	3042	870
	642	392
	815	22
	224	893
	797	132
	948	778
	3787	393
	3041	871
	744	301
	347	13

Cherub

A golden-haired cherub, beautifully stitched on cream evenweave fabric, makes a card to be cherished long after Christmas is over.

p.104), work the design in cross stitch using two strands of embroidery thread. Each square represents one cross stitch over two threads of fabric each way. Where squares are shown divided diagonally, with half in one colour and half in another, work three-quarter and quarter cross stitches (see p.105). When all the cross stitching is complete, add the features in back stitch and satin stitch using one strand of embroidery thread in the colours shown in the chart.

Press the work on the reverse using a hot iron setting (see p.106), then make up the card following the instructions given on p.106. For an extra decorative touch, use a gold pen to draw a narrow border around the the aperture of the card.

	DMC	Anchor
☐	blanc	1
■	793	176
▨	223	895
■	414	235
▨	950	4146
▨	453	231
▨	948	778
▨	415	398
▨	3047	886
▨	3046	887
■	3045	888
	background fabric	

Measurements
The actual design measures 9.5 x 7cm (3¾ x 2¾in)

Materials
• Piece of cream 28-count evenweave fabric measuring 24 x 21cm (9½ x 8¼in)
• DMC or Anchor stranded embroidery cotton, one skein each of the colours shown in the chart
• Tapestry needle, size 26
• Dark-green cardboard mount with square aperture measuring 9.6 x 9.6cm (3¾ x 3¾in)
• Gold pen

To make up
Following the chart and beginning centrally (see

Children in Snow

Playing in the snow is most children's idea of a happy time at Christmas. Make this card for a family with active youngsters like the ones depicted here.

Measurements
The actual design measures 10.25 x 8cm
(4 x 3⅛in)

Materials
• Piece of white 16-count aida fabric measuring 25 x 23cm (10 x 9in)
• DMC or Anchor stranded embroidery cotton, one skein each of the colours shown in the chart
• Tapestry needle, size 24
• Dark-blue cardboard mount with rectangular aperture measuring 12.25 x 9.5cm (4¾ x 3¾in)

To make up
Following the chart and beginning centrally (see p.104), work the design in cross stitch using two strands of embroidery thread. Each square represents one cross stitch. When all the cross stitching is complete, add the fine outlines on the children's boots and the boy's arms in back stitch using one strand of embroidery thread in light gray. This gives the impression of areas of snow. Work the outline of the boy's sleeve in dark gray.

Press the completed work on the reverse using a hot iron setting (see p.106), then make up the card following the instructions given on p.106. For a decorative mount, cut a piece of firm red paper to show just inside the aperture of the card mount as a contrast to the blue.

	DMC	Anchor		DMC	Anchor
■	347	13	■	3328	10
■	317	400	■	826	161
▨	725	306	▨	background fabric	
▨	3774	778			

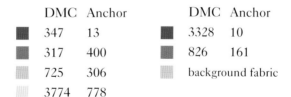

Candlelit Tree

Simply decorated with white candles, this Christmas tree looks fresh from the forest. It is worked on gray-green aida fabric and is mounted in a deep spruce-green card to tone with the tree colours.

To make up

Following the chart and beginning centrally (see p.104), work the design in cross stitch using two strands of embroidery thread. Each square represents one cross stitch.

Press the completed work on the reverse using a hot iron setting (see p.106), then make up the card following the instructions given on p.106.

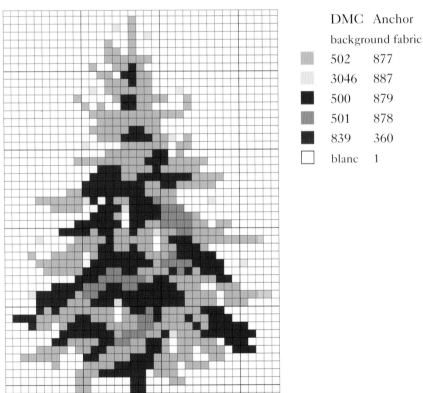

DMC	Anchor
background fabric	
502	877
3046	887
500	879
501	878
839	360
blanc	1

Measurements

The actual design measures 6 x 9.5cm (2⅜ x 3¾in)

Materials

• Piece of light gray-green 14-count aida fabric measuring 21 x 24cm (8¼ x 9½in)
• DMC or Anchor stranded embroidery cotton, one skein each of the colours shown in the chart
• Tapestry needle, size 24
• Dark-green cardboard mount with oval aperture measuring 8 x 10.5cm (3⅛ x 4⅛in)

Boy with Snowball

Every boy delights in throwing snowballs at unwary passers-by and this little lad, poised ready for action, is no exception. He is simple to stitch on aida fabric.

Measurements

The actual design measures 5.5 x 7.5cm (2⅛ x 3in)

Materials

• Piece of white 14-count aida fabric measuring 15 x 17cm (6 x 6¾in)
• DMC or Anchor stranded embroidery cotton, one skein each of the colours shown in the chart
• Tapestry needle, size 24
• Holly-green cardboard mount with rectangular aperture measuring 5.75 x 8cm (2¼ x 3¼in)

To make up

Following the chart and beginning centrally (see p.104), work the design in cross stitch using two strands of embroidery thread. Each square represents one cross stitch. When all the cross stitching is complete, outline the boy's clothes and the snowball in back stitch using one strand of embroidery thread in the colours shown in the chart. Add the boy's features in back stitch and straight stitches in the same way.

Press the completed work on the reverse using a hot iron setting (see p.106), then make up the card following the instructions given on p.106.

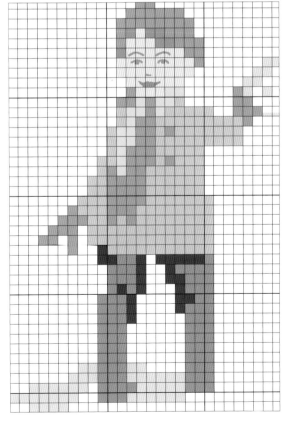

	DMC	Anchor
	223	895
	931	921
	930	922
	341	117
	598	167
	background fabric	
	415	398
	948	778
	611	898
	597	168

The Sleigh Ride

This atmospheric scene has a Victorian feel to it. The young girl, well muffled against the snow, is transporting her Christmas tree home in style.

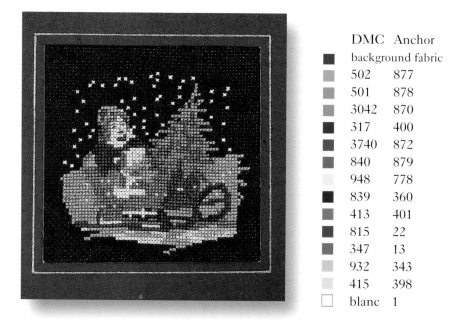

DMC	Anchor
background fabric	
502	877
501	878
3042	870
317	400
3740	872
840	879
948	778
839	360
413	401
815	22
347	13
932	343
415	398
blanc	1

Measurements
The actual design measures 8.5cm (3⅜in) square

Materials
• Piece of dark-blue 18-count aida fabric measuring 23cm (9in) square
• DMC or Anchor stranded embroidery cotton, one skein each of the colours shown in the chart
• Tapestry needle, size 26
• Red cardboard mount with square aperture measuring 9.5 x 9.5cm (3¼ x 3¼in)

To make up
Following the chart and beginning centrally (see p.104), work the design in cross stitch using two strands of embroidery thread. Each square represents one cross stitch. When all the cross stitching is complete, add the small features with straight stitches using one strand of embroidery thread in the colours shown in the chart.

Press the completed work on the reverse using a hot iron setting (see p.106), then mount the card following the instructions given on p.106.

Robin Redbreast

A robin is everyone's favourite winter bird with its cheery red breast, and it makes a perfect motif for a special Christmas card.

strands of embroidery thread. Each square represents one cross stitch. Where squares are shown divided diagonally, with half in one colour and half in another, work three-quarter and quarter cross stitches (see p.105). When all the cross stitching is complete, work the robin's beak and claws with straight stitches in dark gray, using two strands of thread. Work the eye as a circle of back stitches in dark gray with a tiny white straight stitch in the middle, using one strand of thread.

Press the completed work on the reverse using a hot iron setting (see p.106), then make up the card following the instructions given on p.106.

Measurements
The actual design measures 5.25 x 5.75cm (2⅛ x 2¼in)

Materials
• Piece of gray-brown 16-count aida fabric measuring 20 x 20cm (8 x 8in)
• DMC or Anchor stranded embroidery cotton, one skein each of the colours shown in the chart
• Tapestry needle, size 24
• Cardboard mount with circular aperture measuring 8cm (3⅛in) in diameter

To make up
Following the chart and beginning centrally (see p.104), work the design in cross stitch using two

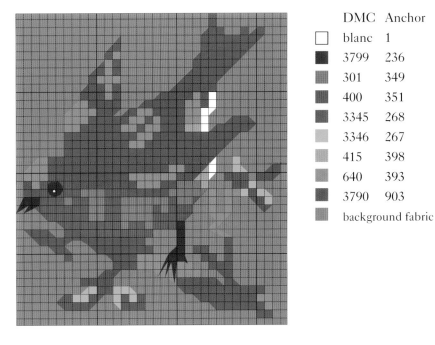

	DMC	Anchor
☐	blanc	1
◼	3799	236
◼	301	349
◼	400	351
◼	3345	268
◼	3346	267
◼	415	398
◼	640	393
◼	3790	903
◼	background fabric	

Father Christmas

This card will be proudly displayed year after year. The colourful figure of Father Christmas is very finely worked to bring out the details on his fur-trimmed robe.

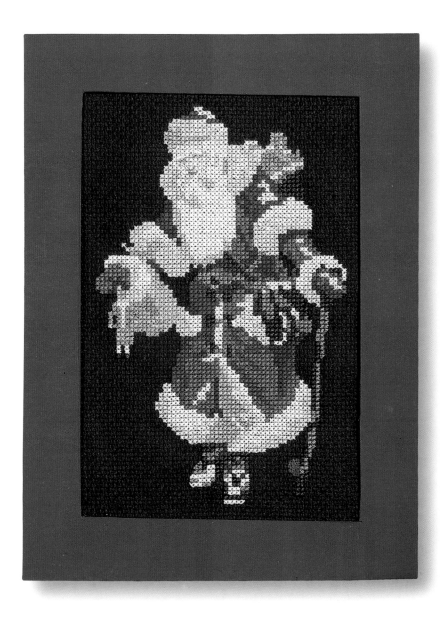

Measurements
The actual design measures 8.5 x 13cm (3⅜ x 5in)

Materials for each decoration
• Piece of dark-blue 18-count aida fabric measuring 23 x 28cm (9 x 11in)
• DMC or Anchor stranded embroidery cotton, one skein each of the colours shown in the chart
• Tapestry needle, size 26
• Red cardboard mount with rectangular aperture measuring 9.5 x 14cm (3¾ x 5½in)

To make up
Following the chart opposite and beginning centrally (see p.104), work the design in cross stitch using two strands of embroidery thread. Each square represents one cross stitch. Where squares are shown divided diagonally, with half in one colour and half in another colour, work three-quarter cross stitches (see p.105). When all the cross stitching is complete, add the facial features in back stitch and straight stitches using a single strand of embroidery thread in the colours shown in the chart.

Press the completed work on the reverse side using a hot iron setting (see p.106), then make up the cardboard mount following the instructions given on p.106.

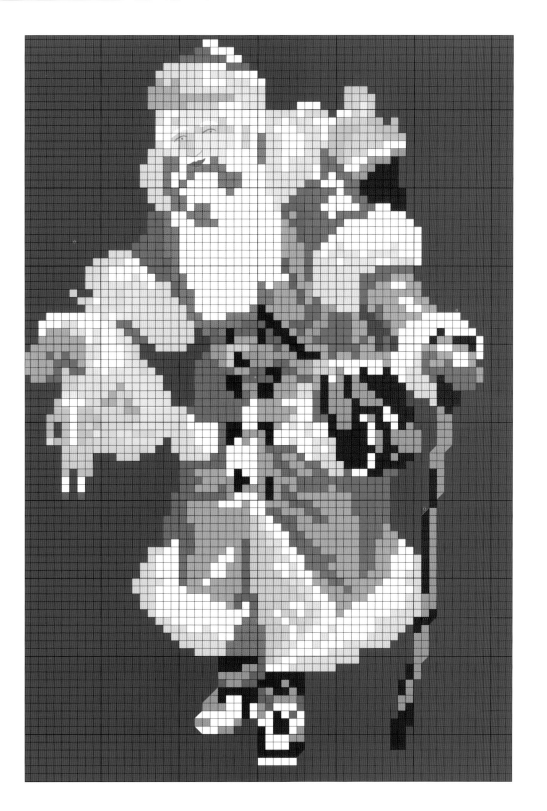

DMC	Anchor
background fabric	
347	13
453	231
452	232
680	901
950	4146
948	778
813	160
3042	870
926	850
415	398
815	22
3328	10
827	9159
838	380
840	379
977	313
blanc	1

Snowdrops

A cluster of snowdrops lift their delicate heads to herald the coming of spring. The deep-blue background throws the pale flowers into relief.

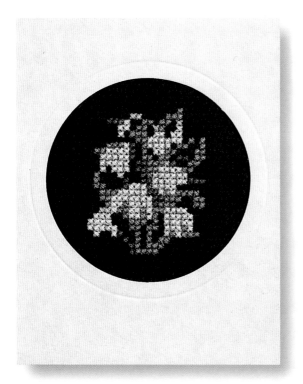

Measurements
The actual design measures 3.75 x 4.5cm (1½ x 1¾in)

Materials for each decoration
• Piece of dark-blue 18-count aida fabric measuring 18 x 19cm (7 x 7½in)
• DMC or Anchor stranded embroidery cotton, one skein each of the colours shown in the chart
• Tapestry needle, size 26

• Cream cardboard mount with circular aperture measuring 6.5cm (2½in) in diameter

To make up
Following the chart and beginning centrally (see p.104), work the design in cross stitch using two strands of embroidery thread. Each square represents one cross stitch.

Press the completed work on the reverse side using a hot iron setting (see p.106), then make up the gift tag following the instructions given on p.106.

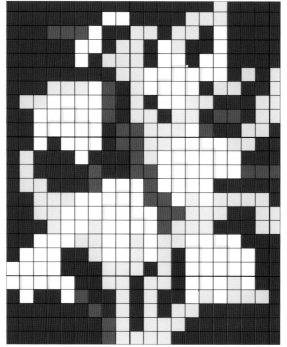

	DMC	Anchor
☐	blanc	1
■	501	878
■	504	875
■	926	850
■	background fabric	

Christmas Bells

Bells ringing out the joyous message on Christmas morning are apt motifs for this gift tag. The bells are shaded to create a three-dimensional effect.

Measurements

The actual design measures 4.5 x 3cm (1¾ x 1¼in)

Materials

• Piece of mid-blue 14-count aida fabric measuring 9 x 8cm (7 x 7in)
• DMC or Anchor stranded embroidery cotton, one skein each of the colours shown in the chart
• Tapestry needle, size 24
• Red cardboard mount with circular aperture measuring 6.5cm (2½in) in diameter

To make up

Following the chart and beginning centrally (see p.104), work the bell design in cross stitch using two strands of embroidery thread. Each square represents one cross stitch. Where squares are shown divided diagonally, with half in one colour and half in another colour, work three-quarter and quarter cross stitches (see p.105). When all the cross stitching is complete, outline the bells in back stitch using a single strand of embroidery thread in dark gray.

Press the completed work on the reverse using a hot iron setting (see p.106), then make up the gift tag following the instructions given on p.106.

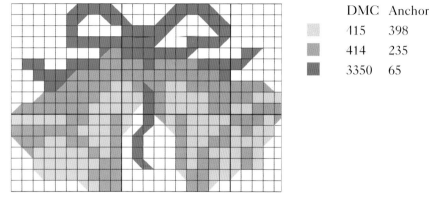

	DMC	Anchor
	415	398
	414	235
	3350	65

Fir Tree and Star Tags

These small gift tags would make ideal projects for a beginner. The motifs would also look attractive worked on 11-count aida fabric as a small card.

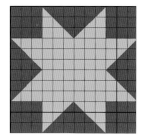

DMC   Anchor

☐ gold thread
■ background fabric

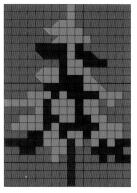

DMC   Anchor

	DMC	Anchor
■	839	360
■	500	879
■	501	878
■	background fabric	

Measurements

The star measures 2.25cm (⅞in) square; the fir tree measures 3 x 4.25cm (1⅛ x 1⅝in)

Materials

For the star, you will need:

• Piece of red 14-count aida fabric measuring 10cm (4in) square
• One reel of DMC or Anchor gold thread
• Tapestry needle, size 24
• Holly-green gift tag with oval aperture measuring 3 x 6cm (1¼ x 2¼in)

For the fir tree, you will need:

• Piece of red 14-count aida fabric measuring 18 x 19cm (7 x 7½in)
• DMC or Anchor stranded embroidery cotton, one skein each of the colours shown in the chart
• Tapestry needle, size 24

• Dark-green gift tag with rectangular aperture measuring 3.25 x 5.75cm (1¼ x 2¼in)

To make up

Following the charts, work the designs in cross stitch. Each square represents one cross stitch. Where squares are shown divided diagonally, with half in one colour and half in another, work three-quarter stitches (see p.105). When all the cross stitching is complete, outline the horizontal and vertical edges of the star with back stitch.

Press the completed works on the reverse using a hot iron setting (see p.106), then make up the gift tags following the instructions given on p.106.

Candle and Goose Tags

These miniature gift tags will take only a matter of minutes to stitch. Even though the designs are simple to work, they are both very lifelike.

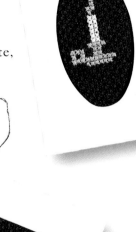

Measurements

The candle measures 2 x 3cm (¾ x 1¼in); the goose measures 3 x 3.5cm (1¼ x 1⅜in)

Materials

For the candle, you will need:
- Piece of dark-blue 14-count aida fabric measuring 10 x 11cm (4 x 4¼in)
- DMC or Anchor stranded embroidery cotton, one skein each of the colours shown in the chart
- Tapestry needle, size 24
- Cream gift tag with oval aperture measuring 3 x 6cm (1¼ x 2¼in)

For the goose, you will need:
- Piece of dark-blue 14-count aida fabric measuring 18cm (7in) square
- DMC or Anchor stranded embroidery cotton, one skein each of the colours shown in the chart
- Tapestry needle, size 24
- Cream gift tag with rectangular aperture measuring 3.25 x 5.75cm (1¼ x 2¼in)

To make up

Following the charts and beginning centrally (see p.104), work the goose and candle designs in cross stitch using two strands of embroidery thread. Each square represents one cross stitch. Where squares are shown divided diagonally, with half the square in one colour and half the square in another colour, work three-quarter cross stitches (see p.105).

When all the cross stitching is complete, work the goose's beak and feet with straight stitches, following the shapes shown on the charts. Finally, add the eye with a tiny straight stitch in dark gray, using a single strand of embroidery thread.

Press the completed works on the reverse using a hot iron setting (see p.106). Mount the gift tags following the instructions given on p.106, then attach a small ribbon loop to the top for hanging.

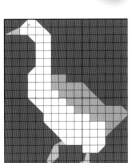

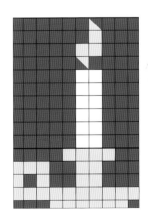

DMC	Anchor
blanc	1
3046	887
background fabric	

DMC	Anchor
blanc	1
414	235
402	347
background fabric	

P ICTURES

Christmas Scenes

Cross stitch is an excellent medium for creating pictures to give a true touch of lively originality to any room at Christmas time. Not only suitable for walls, they can also brighten up a mantelpiece, catch the eye in a window, or even lend unusual seasonal charm to a door. For a peaceful, quiet antidote to all the Christmas glitter, frame your picture in plain or pale-coloured wood; for a more festive feel, try a bright, Christmassy red or green frame, or decorate a plain-coloured frame with just a touch of gold paint.

The five Christmas pictures in this chapter can be enjoyed at any time of the year. If you are too busy to make them in time for Christmas, they can be completed in the spring or summer and either displayed immediately or saved until the following Christmas season. The largest and most time-consuming of the designs is the picture of the boys sledging, but I think the result is well worth the time and effort required to make it. On the other hand, I have designed "Christmas Morning" and "Dear Father Christmas" with large blocks of single colours; this makes them much quicker and easier to work. The "Glad Tidings" picture is the smallest design, and portrays five children out carol singing on a crisp, snowy moonlit night, clustered around a lantern which is shedding a golden glow on the snowy ground. "The Holly Bough" has a lovely nostalgic feel about it and, in fact, was adapted from a cut-out in a child's scrapbook compiled many years ago. My elderly neighbour had

lovingly filled it as a child, and her son gave it to me when she died. The contents have provided much of the inspiration for this book, with their Victorian scraps and delightful old magazine cuttings. Christmas seems to have been the favourite time of year for that little girl long ago, judging from the recurring themes of Father Christmas, children with stockings and snowball fights – just as it is so special for many children today.

All these designs for pictures are very versatile, as parts of them can be taken out and made up as cards or smaller pictures. For example, the boy holding the lantern in the "Glad Tidings" picture could be worked on his own, or the whole group of carol-singing children could be stitched but the background left white. The boy throwing a snowball in the sledging picture is another example of a suitable motif to use alone, and the little puppy in the "Christmas Morning" picture would

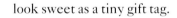

look sweet as a tiny gift tag.

If you prefer, the designs can be worked on aida fabric rather than on the evenweave fabric I have chosen. On 14-count aida fabric, they will work up approximately the same size as the pictures shown, but on 11-count aida they will come up larger, and on 16- or 18-count aida they will be smaller. To ring the changes, you could use your artistic skills to work the designs in different colours. For example, it would be fun to choose different shades for the children's clothes.

Glad Tidings

Impress close friends or relatives with a miniature picture stitched especially for them.
This festive embroidery depicts children practising their carol singing.

Measurements

The actual design measures 11 x 14.5cm
(4½ x 5⅛in)

Materials

• Piece of white 27-count evenweave fabric
measuring 21 x 24cm (8½ x 9½in)
• DMC or Anchor stranded embroidery cotton,
one skein each of the colours shown in the chart
• Tapestry needle, size 26
• Piece of acid-free backing cardboard
measuring 12 x 15.5cm (4¾ x 6in)
• Strong thread for lacing
• Picture frame

To make up

Following the chart opposite, beginning centrally
(see p.104), work the design in cross stitch using
two strands of embroidery thread. Each square
represents one cross stitch worked over two fabric
threads. When all the cross stitching is complete,
add the outlining on the light-brown coat and the
dark-gray coat in back stitch using one strand of
embroidery thread in the colours shown in the
chart. Work the children's features in back stitch
and straight stitches in the same way.

Press the completed work on the reverse using
a hot iron setting (see p.106). To finish the
picture, either stretch the embroidery yourself
over stiff acid-free backing cardboard (see p.106)
and mount it in a shop-bought frame, or take it to
a picture framer to be professionally stretched
and framed.

DMC	Anchor
336	149
501	878
725	306
610	889
632	936
948	778
3752	976
950	4146
3041	871
932	343
3042	870
3354	74
3721	896
407	914
3799	236
931	921
221	897
	background fabric

The Holly Bough

This picture has a delightful period charm and would be fun to make as a present. Mount it in a frame stained with soft shades of green to echo the colours of the embroidery.

Measurements
The actual design measures 18.5 x 19cm (7¼ x 7½in)

Materials
• Piece of white 27-count evenweave fabric measuring 35cm (14in) square
• DMC or Anchor stranded embroidery cotton, one skein each of the colours shown in the chart
• Tapestry needle, size 26
• Piece of acid-free backing cardboard measuring 20 x 21cm (8 x 8¼in)
• Strong thread for lacing
• Picture frame

To make up
Following the chart opposite and beginning centrally (see p.104), work the design in cross stitch using two strands of embroidery thread. Each square represents one cross stitch worked over two fabric threads each way. Where squares are shown divided diagonally, with half in one colour and half in another, work three-quarter stitches (see p.105). When the cross stitching is complete, add the boy's features in back stitch, straight stitch and satin stitch using one strand of embroidery thread in the colours shown in the chart.

Press the work on the reverse using a hot iron setting (see p.106). Finally, stretch the embroidery over stiff acid-free backing cardboard (see p.106) and mount it in a shop-bought frame, or take it to a picture framer to be professionally stretched and framed.

DMC	Anchor		DMC	Anchor		DMC	Anchor
3053	858		224	893		791	178
472	278		640	393		413	401
3362	263		3047	886		background fabric	
347	13		3046	887		816	44
3774	778		792	177			
3790	903		3743	869			

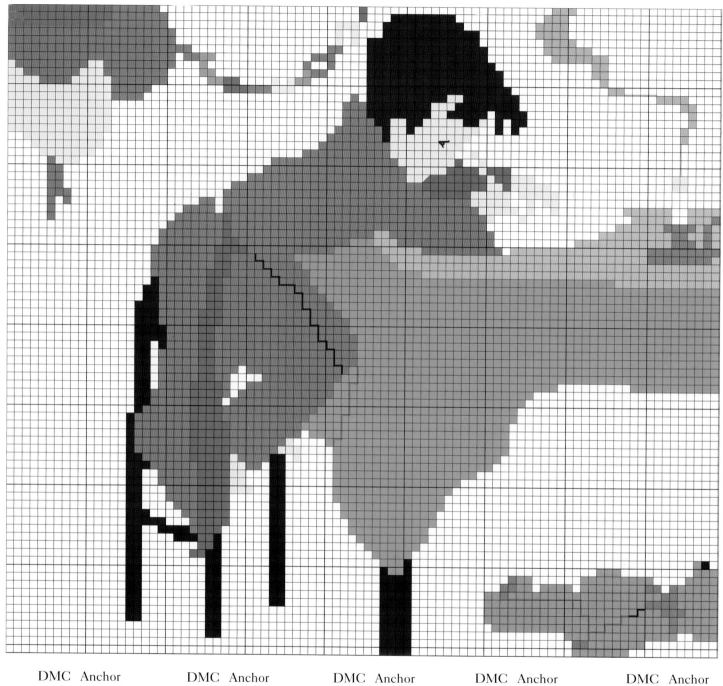

DMC	Anchor		DMC	Anchor		DMC	Anchor		DMC	Anchor		DMC	Anchor
3328	10		347	13		726	295		3041	871		3045	888
561	212		415	398		341	117		3747	120		blanc	1
background fabric			840	379		948	778		3046	887			

Dear Father Christmas

Balloons and paper chains form the background to this delightful picture showing the concentration of a small child as he writes his message to Father Christmas. Mount it in a light-coloured frame to complement the pastel colours of the embroidery.

Measurements

The actual design measures 17.5 x 15.25cm (6⅞ x 6in)

Materials

- Piece of cream 27-count evenweave fabric measuring 28 x 25cm (11 x 10in)
- Tapestry needle, size 26
- DMC or Anchor stranded cotton, one skein each of the colours shown in the chart (opposite)
- Piece of strong acid-free backing board
- Strong thread for lacing
- Picture frame

To make up

Following the chart opposite and beginning centrally (see p.104), work the design in cross stitch using two strands of embroidery thread. Each square represents one cross stitch over two threads of fabric each way. When all the cross stitching is complete, work the boy's eye and the teddy's eye with one tiny straight stitch using one strand of embroidery thread. Add any final features – for example, the detailed work on the boy's pyjamas, the tablecloth, the teddy bear and the candle smoke – with small back stitches in the colours shown in the chart, also using a single strand of embroidery thread.

Press the completed work on the reverse using a hot iron setting (see p.106). To finish the picture, either stretch the embroidery yourself over a piece of stiff acid-free backing cardboard (p.106) and mount it in a shop-bought frame, or take it to a picture framer where you can have it professionally stretched and framed. I have chosen a plain, light wood frame, which blends discreetly with the subtle, pastel shades of the finished embroidery.

Christmas Morning

What could delight a small boy more than a brand new puppy bouncing on his bed on Christmas morning? Simply framed in a plain wooden surround, this picture would look charming in a child's room.

Measurements

The actual design measures 17 x 15cm (6¾ x 6in)

Materials for each decoration

• Piece of cream 27-count evenweave fabric measuring 27 x 25cm (10½ x 10in)
• DMC or Anchor stranded embroidery cotton, one skein each of the colours shown in the chart
• Tapestry needle, size 26
• Piece of strong acid-free backing cardboard
• Strong thread for lacing

To make up

Following the chart opposite and beginning centrally (see p.104), work the design in cross stitch using two strands of embroidery thread. Each square represents one cross stitch worked over two threads of fabric each way. When all the cross stitching is complete, outline the puppy in back stitch using one strand of embroidery thread in the colour shown in the chart. Add the detail on the boy's pyjama sleeve in the same way. Work a few back stitches on the paper chains using the colours shown in the chart. Finally, add the features on the boy's face and the puppy's face with back stitch and straight stitches, again using a single strand of embroidery thread in the colours shown on the chart.

Press the completed work on the reverse using a hot iron setting (see p.106). To finish the picture, either stretch the embroidery yourself over stiff acid-free backing cardboard (see p.106) and mount it in a shop-bought frame, or take it to a picture framer to be professionally stretched and framed.

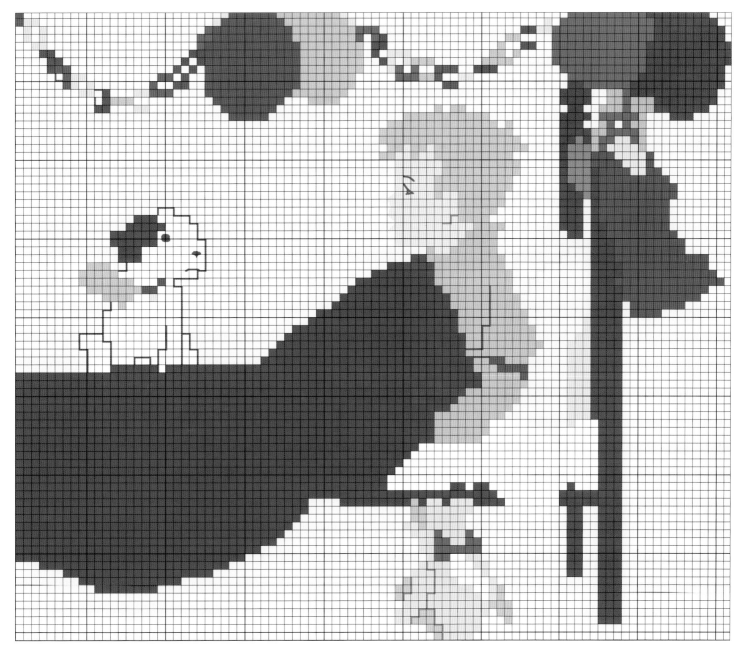

DMC	Anchor		DMC	Anchor		DMC	Anchor		DMC	Anchor		DMC	Anchor
background fabric			3740	872		610	889		727	293		blanc	1
355	341		340	118		3046	887		3768	779		611	898
725	306		924	851		948	778		3047	886			

DMC	Anchor	DMC	Anchor	DMC	Anchor	DMC	Anchor	DMC	Anchor
background fabric		950	4146	677	300	3726	970	415	398
336	149	3790	903	367	216	676	891	blanc	1
932	343	3774	778	315	896	522	860		
640	393	413	401	319	217	312	979		

Boys with Sledge

This picture is ideal for those of you who like to have a large project on the go.
The atmospheric scene will look good in your home long after winter is over.

Measurements
The actual design measures 28 x 24cm (11 x 9½in)

Materials
• Piece of light-blue 28-count evenweave fabric measuring 41 x 36cm (16 x 14 in)

• DMC or Anchor stranded embroidery cotton, one skein each of the colours shown in the chart
• Tapestry needle, size 26
• Piece of acid-free backing cardboard measuring 29.5 x 26cm (11½ x 10¼in)
• Strong thread for lacing
• Picture frame

To make up
Following the chart opposite and beginning centrally (see p.104), work the design in cross stitch using two strands of embroidery thread. Each square represents one cross stitch worked over two threads of fabric each way. When all the cross stitching is complete, add the boys' eyes, eyebrows and nostrils in back stitch, satin stitch and tiny straight stitches using one strand of embroidery thread in the colour shown in the chart. Work the boys' mouths in back stitch and satin stitch using two strands of thread.

Press the completed work on the reverse using a hot iron setting (see p.106). To finish the picture, either stretch the embroidery yourself over stiff acid-free backing cardboard (see p.106) and mount it in a shop-bought frame, or take it to a picture framer and have it professionally stretched and framed.

DECORATIONS

*O*rnaments

In most households, the same Christmas decorations are brought out year after year and become an integral part of the traditional festivities, so I think it is well worth spending some time and effort to create your own hand-made decorations making use of the cross-stitch designs featured in this chapter. It is so pleasurable getting the old box of decorations down from the loft or cupboard each year and rediscovering the well-loved items inside as you deck the tree in that happy annual ritual. We still have some decorations at home that my husband's family had when he was a child, and the ones in this book, if packed away carefully after Christmas, should last for many years and can be passed down to your children. It's a heart-warming thought that in years to come, future generations of children may be eagerly rummaging in the decorations box and getting out the familiar treasures hand-crafted by their grandmother or great-grandmother.

One good thing about these cross-stitch decorations, apart from the fact that you can make them yourself, is that they don't break if dropped or knocked off the tree by a lively child or an inquisitive kitten. In fact, the only danger you would have to think about protecting them against would be the possibility of falling prey to moths while stored away each year between Christmases! The tree decorations featured in this chapter – the baubles, miniature sacks and stockings – need not be restricted to the Christmas tree. They can also be hung on branches brought in to decorate your home, such as a classic bough of holly, bare, barky branches or fresh-smelling evergreen, adding a touch of colour and opulence to your usual seasonal decorations.

Any of the baubles shown here, with their gold edging glinting in the light, will look wonderful on your tree or Christmas foliage. The designs could also be used as cards, or, worked larger on 14-count aida fabric, as pictures. On the other hand, to add further to the range of possibilities, several of the designs from the cards chapter could be made up as tree baubles.

The two tiny tree stockings are made of rich-looking velvet, with gold lace and braid, but they could equally well be made up in brocade or some other luxurious fabric. Fill them with tiny gifts, sweets or chocolates before hanging them on the tree. The two tree sacks are shamelessly glossy and decadent-looking, with their shiny red and blue fabric, "shot" ribbon, and row of glittery beads adorning the lower edge. These can also be made in velvet or brocade if preferred and, like the stockings, should be filled with goodies – just a few, so they are not too heavy.

Mantelpiece borders are another lovely way to decorate your house. If you want a spectacular effect that can be produced in a short time, choose the snowman decoration. You need only stitch one motif in the middle, sew on a length of shiny fringing, and attach a couple of bows. If you have more time, you can repeat the snowman design along the length of the border. The angels design will take longer to complete, but will look glorious, and the angels can also be made up as pictures.

Brunette Cherub Bauble

The brunette version of the cherub is just as attractive as the blond one. They would make an enchanting pair for your tree, or to give as scented sachets to a special friend.

Measurements
The decoration measures 7.5 x 8.5cm (3 x 3⅜in)

Materials
• Piece of white or cream 18-count aida fabric measuring 17 x 18cm (6¾ x 7in)
• DMC or Anchor stranded embroidery cotton, one skein each of the colours shown in the chart
• Reel of DMC gold thread
• Tapestry needle, size 26
• Piece of deep-blue felt measuring 9 x 9.5cm (3½ x 3¾in)
• Piece of 2.5cm-(1in-)thick wadding measuring 9 x 9.5cm (3½ x 3¾in)
• Narrow twisted cord or braid 38cm (15in) in length
• Small piece of tracing paper

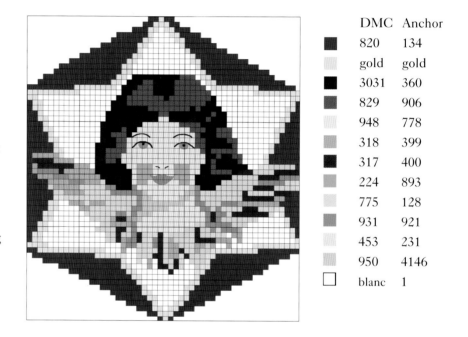

	DMC	Anchor
	820	134
	gold	gold
	3031	360
	829	906
	948	778
	318	399
	317	400
	224	893
	775	128
	931	921
	453	231
	950	4146
	blanc	1

To make up
Following the chart and beginning centrally (see p.104), work the design in cross stitch using two strands of embroidery thread. Each square represents one cross stitch. When all the cross stitching is complete, add the cherub's features in back stitch and satin stitch using one strand of embroidery thread in the colours shown in the chart.

Press the completed work on the reverse using a hot iron setting (see p.104), then make up the bauble following the instructions given on p.106.

Blonde Cherub Bauble

This angelic cherub would make an adorable keepsake. To make the decoration even more special, why not fill it with pot pourri to scent your Christmas tree?

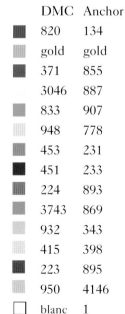

Measurements
The decoration measures 7.5 x 8.5cm (3 x 3 ⅜in)

Materials
• Piece of white or cream 18-count aida fabric measuring 17 x 18cm (6¾ x 7in)
• DMC or Anchor stranded embroidery cotton, one skein each of the colours shown in the chart (opposite)
• Reel of DMC or Anchor gold thread
• Tapestry needle, size 26
• Piece of deep-blue felt measuring 9 x 9.5cm (3½ x 3¾in)
• Piece of 2.5cm-(1in-)thick wadding measuring 9 x 9.5cm (3½cm x 3¾in)
• Narrow twisted cord or braid 38cm (15in) in length
• Small piece of tracing paper

To make up
Following the chart and beginning centrally (see p.104), work the design in cross stitch using two strands of embroidery thread. Each square represents one cross stitch. When all the cross stitching is complete, add the cherub's features in back stitch and satin stitch using one strand of embroidery thread in the colours shown in the chart.

Press the completed work on the reverse using a hot iron setting (see p.106), then make up the decoration following the instructions that are given on p.106.

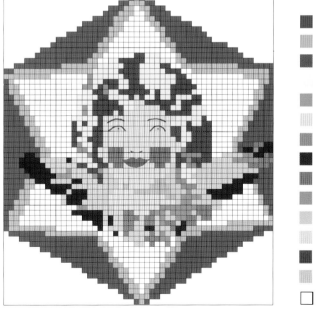

	DMC	Anchor
■	820	134
	gold	gold
■	371	855
	3046	887
■	833	907
	948	778
■	453	231
■	451	233
■	224	893
■	3743	869
■	932	343
■	415	398
■	223	895
	950	4146
☐	blanc	1

Musical Angel Bauble

Traditionally, angels played sweet music on gold-stringed harps. This elaborate design was reproduced from an original Victorian Christmas card discovered in an antique shop.

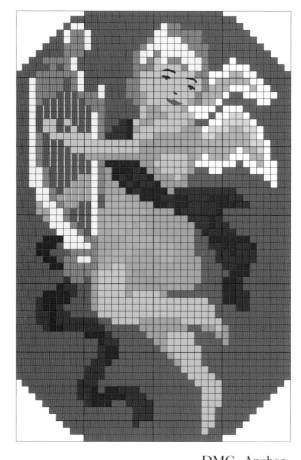

Measurements

The tree decoration measures 6 x 10cm (2¼ x 4in)

Materials

- Piece of cream or gray 16-count aida fabric measuring 15 x 20cm (6 x 8in)
- DMC or Anchor stranded embroidery cotton, one skein each of the colours shown in the chart
- Scrap of brown for eyes
- Reel of DMC gold thread for harp strings
- Tapestry needle, size 26
- Piece of 2.5cm-(1in-)thick wadding measuring 6 x 10cm (2¼ x 4in)
- Piece of felt measuring 6 x 10cm (2¼ x 4in)
- Length of narrow twisted cord measuring 40cm (16in)
- Tracing paper

To make up

Following the chart and beginning centrally (see p.104), work the design in cross stitch using two strands of embroidery thread. Each square represents one cross stitch. When all the cross stitching is complete, add the features in back stitch, straight stitches and satin stitch using one strand of embroidery thread in the colours shown in the chart. The strings of the harp are long straight stitches in gold thread.

Press the completed work on the reverse side using a hot iron setting (see p.106), then make up the decoration following the instructions that are given on p.106.

	DMC	Anchor
	blanc	1
	3047	886
	3768	779
	924	851
	798	131
	796	133
	928	847
	950	4146
	300	352
	415	398
	948	778
	372	854
	gold	gold
	347	13

Young Girl Bauble

Looking her best in her fur-trimmed winter outfit, this small girl is laden with gifts and Christmas foliage. She'll make a delightful addition to your tree decorations.

Measurements

The tree decoration measures 6 x 10cm (2¼ x 4in)

Materials

• Piece of cream or gray 16-count aida fabric measuring 15 x 20cm (6 x 8in)
• DMC or Anchor stranded embroidery cotton, one skein each of the colours shown in the chart
• Tapestry needle, size 26
• Piece of 2.5cm-(1in-)thick wadding measuring 6 x 10cm (2¼ x 4in)
• Piece of felt measuring 6 x 10cm (2¼ x 4in)
• Length of narrow twisted cord measuring 40cm (16in)
• Tracing paper

To make up

Following the chart and beginning centrally (see p.104), work the design in cross stitch using two strands of embroidery thread. Each square represents one cross stitch. Where squares are shown divided diagonally, with half in one colour and half in another, work three-quarter and quarter cross stitches (see p.105). When all the cross stitching is complete, add the parcel details in back stitch using one strand of embroidery thread in the colour shown in the chart. Add the girl's features in back stitch and tiny straight stitches, also using a single strand of thread in the colours shown in the chart.

Press the completed work on the reverse using a hot iron setting (see p.106), then make up the decoration following the instructions that are given on p.106.

	DMC	Anchor
☐	blanc	1
■	3781	905
▨	640	393
▨	224	893
▨	948	778
▨	3046	887
▨	415	398
▨	988	243
▨	319	217
▨	3328	10
▨	347	13
■	336	149

Christmas Turkey Bauble

*Here is one turkey that won't be eaten for Christmas! Stitch him in all his splendour
and display him on your tree.*

Measurements

The actual design measures 8 x 10 cm (3¼ x 4in)

Materials

• Piece of gray 14-count aida fabric measuring 18 x 20cm (7 x 8 in)
• DMC or Anchor stranded embroidery cotton, one skein each of the colours shown in the chart
• Scrap of dark-gray cotton for eye
• Tapestry needle, size 24
• Piece of 2.5cm-(1in-)thick wadding measuring 8 x 10cm (3¼ x 4in)
• Piece of felt measuring 8 x 10cm (3¼ x 4in)
• Length of narrow twisted cotton measuring 45cm (17½in)
• Tracing paper

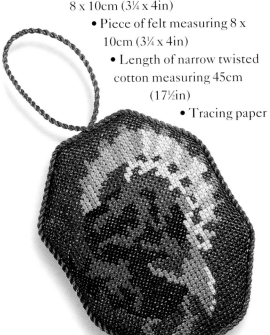

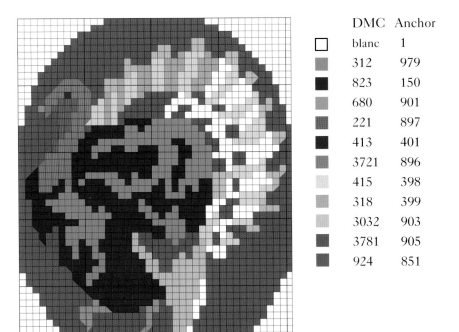

	DMC	Anchor
	blanc	1
	312	979
	823	150
	680	901
	221	897
	413	401
	3721	896
	415	398
	318	399
	3032	903
	3781	905
	924	851

To make up

Following the chart and beginning centrally (see p.104), work the design in cross stitch using two strands of embroidery thread. Each square represents one cross stitch. Where squares are shown divided diagonally, with half in one colour and half in another, work three-quarter and quarter cross stitches (see p.105).

Press the completed work on the reverse using a hot iron setting (see p.106), then make up the decoration following the instructions on p.106.

Christmas Pudding Bauble

No Christmas is complete without a traditional round pudding studded with raisins and topped with a holly sprig. Have fun making this one to decorate your tree.

Measurements
The actual design measures 8 x 7.5cm (3¼ x 3in)

Materials
• Piece of cream 14-count aida fabric measuring 18 x 18cm (7 x 7cm)
• DMC or Anchor stranded embroidery cotton, one skein each of the colours shown in the chart
• Tapestry needle, size 26
• Piece of 2.5cm-(1in-)thick wadding measuring 8 x 7.5cm (3¼ x 3in)
• Piece of felt measuring 8 x 8cm (3¼ x 3¼in)
• Length of narrow twisted cord measuring 40cm (16in)
• Tracing paper

To make up
Following the chart and beginning centrally (see p.104), work the design in cross stitch using two strands of embroidery thread. Each square represents one cross stitch. Where squares are shown divided diagonally, with half in one colour and half in another, work three-quarter and quarter cross stitches (see p.105).

Press the completed work on the reverse side using a hot iron setting (see p.106), then make up the decoration following the instructions that are given on p.106.

	DMC	Anchor
	blanc	1
	415	398
	3371	382
	839	360
	433	371
	347	13
	501	878
	502	877
	676	891

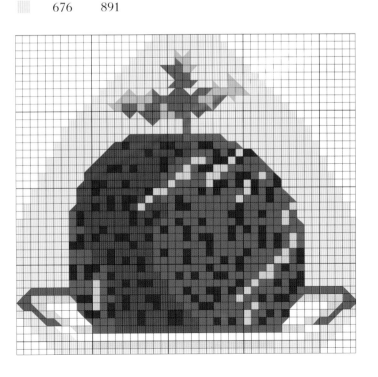

Snowman Tree Sack

Tiny sacks made from rich, glittery fabric and jewel-like beads will add a magical touch to your tree. Fill them with sweets or pot pourri before hanging them up.

Measurements

The actual design measures 4 x 6.25cm (1½ x 2½in). The bag measures 9 x 15cm (3½ x 6in)

Materials

• Piece of blue 14-count aida fabric measuring 14 x 16cm (5½ x 6¼in)
• DMC or Anchor stranded embroidery cotton, one skein each of the colours shown in the chart
• Tapestry needle, size 24
• Piece of fabric measuring 12 x 33cm (4¾ x 13in)
• Beads, braid or lace for trimming
• Piece of 7.5cm-(3in-)wide ribbon 50cm (20in) in length

To make up

Following the chart and beginning centrally (see p.104), work the design in cross stitch using two strands of embroidery thread. Each square represents one cross stitch. Where squares are shown divided diagonally, with half in one colour and half in another, work three-quarter cross stitches (see p.105). When all the cross stitching is complete, outline the snowman in back stitch using one strand of embroidery thread in the colour shown in the chart. Work his features in the same way.

Press the completed work on the reverse using a hot iron setting (see p.106), then make up the tree bag following the instructions given on p.106.

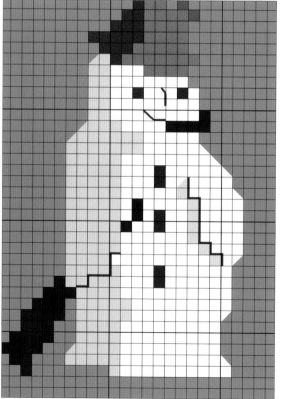

DMC	Anchor
background fabric	
3799	236
414	235
415	398
839	360
blanc	1
561	212
347	13

Santa Claus Tree Sack

Ornate red fabric is an appropriate background for Santa on this decorative little bag. Hide a tiny gift inside Santa's sack before tying the shimmering bow.

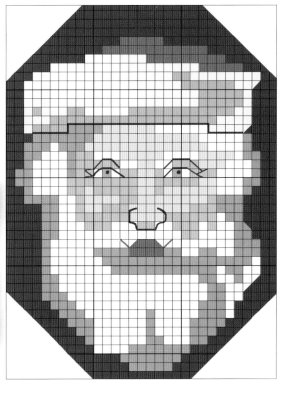

Measurements

The actual design measures 4.75 x 6.5cm (1⅞ x 2½in). The bag measures 9 x 15cm (3½ x 6in)

Materials

• Piece of cream 16-count aida fabric measuring 15 x 17cm (6 x 6¾in)
• DMC or Anchor stranded embroidery cotton, one skein each of the colours shown in the chart
• Tapestry needle, size 24
• Piece of fabric measuring 12 x 33cm (4¾ x 13in)
• Beads, braid or lace for trimming
• Piece of 7.5cm-(3in-)wide ribbon 50cm (20in) in length

To make up

Following the chart and beginning centrally (see p.104), work the design in cross stitch using two strands of embroidery thread. Each square represents one cross stitch. Where squares are shown divided diagonally, with half in one colour and half in another, work three-quarter cross stitches (see p.105). When all the cross stitching is complete, outline the bottom of Santa's hat in back stitch in mid-gray using one strand of thread. Add his features in back stitch, adding two straight stitches for the corners of his mouth, using one strand of embroidery thread in the colours shown in the chart.

	DMC	Anchor
☐	blanc	1
	826	161
	950	4146
	3774	778
	415	398
	644	391
	822	390
	347	13
	300	352

Angel Tree Stocking

Metallic braid and gold cord on midnight-blue velvet give a luxurious feel to this miniature stocking for the Christmas tree. Add a stitched angel to complete the decoration.

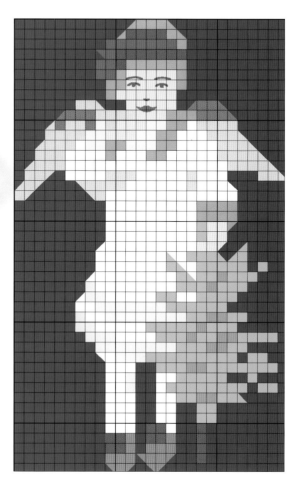

Measurements

The actual design measures 5 x 8.5cm (2 x 3⅜in). The stocking is 12.5cm (5in) high

Materials

• Piece of dark-blue 14-count aida fabric measuring 20 x 23cm (8 x 9in)
• DMC or Anchor stranded embroidery cotton, one skein each of the colours shown in the chart
• Tapestry needle, size 24
• Piece of fabric (velvet, felt, brocade) measuring 32 x 13.5cm (12½ x 5¼in)
• Piece of 2cm-(¾in-)wide braid 20cm (8in) in length
• Length of narrow twisted cord measuring 60cm (23½in)
• Tracing paper

To make up

Following the chart and beginning centrally (see p.104), work the design in cross stitch using two strands of embroidery thread. Each square represents one cross stitch. Where squares are shown divided diagonally, with half in one colour and half in another, work three-quarter cross stitches (see p.105). When all the cross stitching is complete, add the angel's features in back stitch using one strand of embroidery thread in the colours shown in the chart.

Press the completed work on the reverse using a hot iron setting (see p.106), then make up the stocking following the instructions on p.107.

	DMC	Anchor
☐	écru	387
	3042	870
	451	233
	453	231
	948	778
	372	854
	816	44
	370	856
	background fabric	
	501	878
	502	877

Bell Tree Stocking

Garlands and ribbons festoon the bell on this green velvet stocking. Fill it with tiny gifts or chocolates.

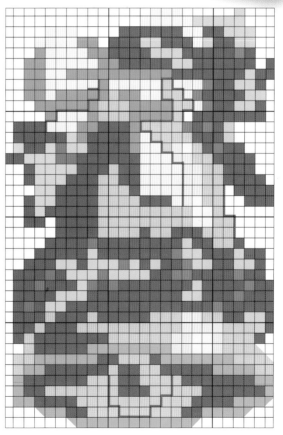

Measurements

The actual design measures 5 x 7cm (2 x 2¾in). The stocking is 12.5cm (5in) high

Materials

• Piece of gray-green 14-count aida fabric measuring 20 x 22cm (8 x 8¾in)
• DMC or Anchor stranded embroidery cotton, one skein each of the colours shown in the chart
• Tapestry needle, size 24
• Piece of fabric (velvet, felt, brocade) measuring 32 x 13.5cm (12½ x 5¼in)
• Piece of 2.5cm-(1in-)wide gold braid 20cm (8in) in length
• Length of narrow twisted cord measuring 60cm (23½in)
• Tracing paper

To make up

Following the chart and beginning centrally (see p.104), work the design in cross stitch using two strands of embroidery thread. Each square represents one cross stitch. Where squares are shown divided diagonally, with half in one colour and half in another, work three-quarter cross stitches (see p.105). When all the cross stitching is complete, work back stitch outlines around the ribbon and part of the bell, using one strand of embroidery thread in the colour in the chart.

Press the completed work on the reverse using a hot iron setting (see p.106), then make up the tree stocking following the instructions on p.107.

DMC	Anchor
869	944
3045	888
347	13
3042	870
319	217
367	216
224	893
background fabric	
435	901
712	926
3046	887

Snowman Mantelpiece Border

This jolly design can be repeated along the length of the border. If you are short of time, you can just stitch it in the middle and decorate the rest with plain or tartan bows.

Measurements

The border is 10cm (4in) high and as long as required

Materials

• Red 15-count aida band measuring 10cm (4in) in width and the length of your mantelpiece
• Gold fringing measuring the same length as the aida band
• DMC or Anchor stranded embroidery cotton, one skein each of the colours shown in the chart
• Tapestry needle, size 24
• Piece of 4cm-(1½in-)wide gold ribbon 61-cm (24in) in length, for bows (optional)

To make up

Following the chart opposite and centering the design on the aida band, work the snowman border in cross stitch using two strands of embroidery thread. Each square represents one cross stitch. The design is 43 squares high and the aida band is 54 squares high; position the upper edge of the design seven squares down from the top of the band, and the lower edge of the design four squares up from the bottom edge of the band. Where squares are shown on the chart divided diagonally, with half in one colour and half in another colour, work three-quarter cross stitches (see p.105). The snowscene design can be repeated along the length of the band, or you could work three designs, one in the the middle and one on each side, equi-distant from the middle and the edges. When all the cross stitching is complete, outline the snowman's arms and head in back stitch and add his features in back stitch, using a single strand of charcoal embroidery thread. Finally, work the children's features with tiny straight stitches using one strand of thread in the colours shown in the chart.

Once the embroidery is complete, press the completed work on the reverse side using a hot iron setting (see p.106), then make up the mantelpiece border as follows. Turn under a 1cm (⅜in) hem all around the raw edges and slipstitch it in place. Attach the gold fringing to the lower edge of the aida band. Finally, cut the gold ribbon into two equal lengths and tie them into neat bows. Attach these to the band on either side of the cross-stitched decoration.

	DMC	Anchor
	background fabric	
	311	148
	3799	236
	948	778
	415	398
	924	851
	839	360
	725	306
	3041	871
	806	169
	blanc	1

Musical Angels Mantelpiece Border

This ruched velvet mantelpiece decoration will add a touch of Victoriana to your fireplace. However, if you have no mantelpiece, the decoration would look just as beautiful draped across a doorway or window frame.

Measurements

Each angel panel measures 18 x 24cm (7 x 9½in)

Materials

• Blue 24-count aida fabric measuring 76 x 44cm (30 x 17¼in)
• DMC or Anchor stranded embroidery cotton, one skein each of the colours shown in the charts (overleaf)
• Tapestry needle, size 24
• Matching felt for backing measuring 36 x 24cm (14¼ x 9½in)
• Piece of 38cm-(15in-)wide deep-blue velvet to fit the length of your mantelpiece
• Decorative braid to fit the length of your mantelpiece
• Narrow twisted cord 1.3m (51in) in length

To make up

Cut the aida fabric widthways into two pieces, each measuring 38 x 44cm (15 x 1 ¼in). Following the charts on pages 58 and 59 and beginning centrally, work one angel in cross stitch on each piece of aida using two strands of embroidery thread. Each square represents one cross stitch. Next, add the angels' features in back stitch and satin stitch using one strand of embroidery thread in the colours shown in the chart.

Press the completed work on the reverse using a hot iron setting (see p.106). Trim each piece of aida fabric to make a panel measuring 22cm (8¾in) along the top, 28cm (11in) along the outside edge and 22cm (8¾in) along the inside edge, completing the shape of the curve. When you are marking the measurements, make sure that the

angels are positioned 5cm (2in) down from the top and 5.5cm (2⅛in) from the inside and outside edges of the panel.

Turn under and stitch a double 1cm (⅜in) hem around the edges of both panels, notching the fabric at the curves. Cut the velvet to measure 40cm (15¾in) deep and the width of your mantelpiece minus 36cm (14¼in) to allow for the panels. Add 2cm (¾in) all around for the hem allowance. Turn under a 1cm (⅜in) hem all around the edges and stitch. To create the ruched effect, run a line of gathering stitches along each side edge. Pull up the gathers to fit the inside edges of the embroidered panels. Slipstitch each panel to the gathered sides of the velvet. Sew braid, lace or beading around the edges of the embroidered panels and along the top of the decoration.

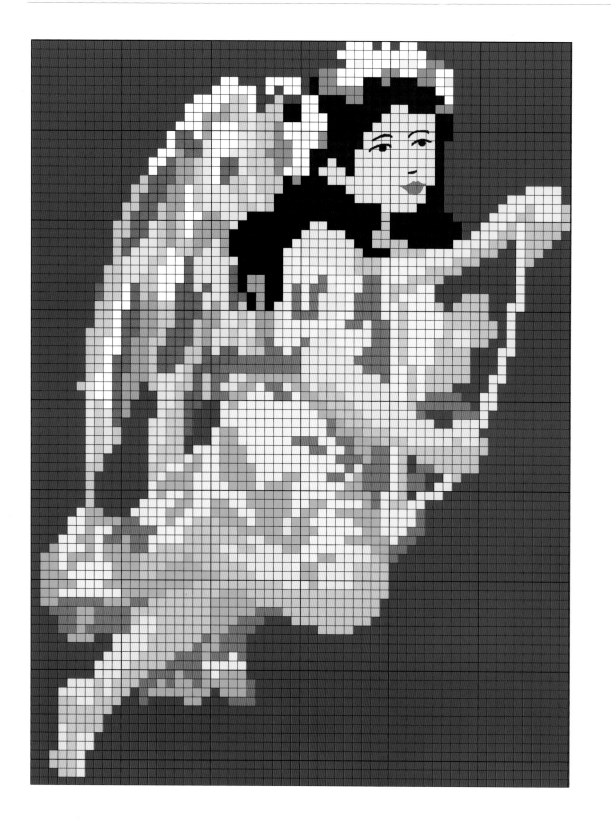

DMC	Anchor
blanc	1
818	48
3733	75
3731	38
3743	869
950	4146
3045	888
648	900
3752	976
948	778
415	398
452	232
838	380
320	215
3046	887
background fabric	

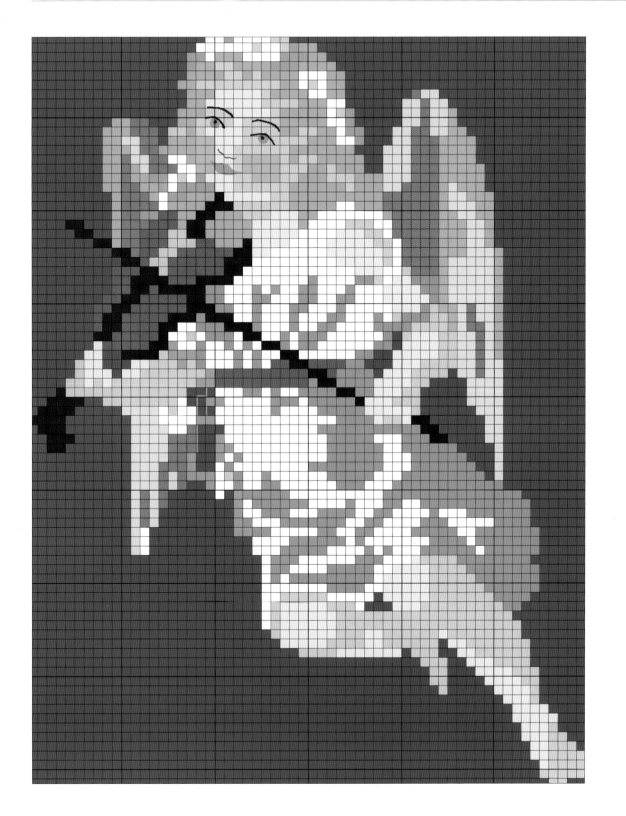

DMC	Anchor
background fabric	
3046	887
320	215
3045	888
948	778
414	235
415	398
950	4146
452	232
224	893
838	380
794	175
801	358
793	176
3041	871
blanc	1
3731	38

GIFTS

*P*resents for All

For all the pleasure of giving gifts to your nearest and dearest each Christmas, it is always a very difficult task trying to think of what to give everybody – a challenge, in fact, that seems to become more demanding with every year that goes by. But if you can allow yourself enough extra time to make those presents, I think you will find the inspiration for unusual cross-stitch gifts for many of your friends and relations in this chapter. Home-made gifts will always be cherished because of the thought and care that have gone into them. Making things for people is a real sign of love.

The twelve gifts that I have designed for this chapter range from the quick, inexpensive and easy-to-make, like the buttons and the bookmark, to the larger, more time-consuming, for example the "Cherubs" cushion, and there are many more possibilities in between. Some of the gifts could easily be personalized by adding the recipient's name to them in a neat cross stitch.

Most of these items are appropriate presents for friends and relatives of either sex. The bookmark, glasses case and paperweight are all very suitable gifts for men, although they will, of course, be much appreciated by women too.

The wallet could be adapted to be more appropriate for a male recipient by substituting another design, such as a goose from the Table Settings chapter or a turkey from the Decorations chapter, for the Christmas rose on the front. For a man with traditional tastes, you could make the wallet in a more subdued shade of thread, with dark ribbon around the edge rather than the bright tartan suggested in my version.

Children will love the useful pencil case and would of course thoroughly enjoy hanging up the Christmas stocking every year. An older child would also appreciate the "Robins" box to keep his or her tiny trinkets and treasures in.

The brooch pillow could be filled with lavender or pot pourri to add a lovely fragrance to a room. This design can also be worked larger on 14-count aida fabric and made up into a full-size pillow. The fob pin design of the little Victorian boy can be used in a locket, too, or made up on 14-count fabric and turned into a greetings card design.

Finally, this chapter also contains two braid designs worked on narrow aida band; these can be wrapped around presents as very special Christmas ribbon or given as presents themselves. The berry braid can be made up in any length and sewn onto items such as the bib on a pair of child's dungarees, the hem of a curtain or the edging of a pillowcase or towel. The star design is rather more fragile than the berry design because of the gold thread and the length of the stitches, so is not so suitable for items which will receive a lot of wear and need frequent washing, but is nonetheless highly decorative.

Christmas Rose Wallet

This cheery wallet with a tartan edging is practical as well as decorative, and will brighten up any gloomy day. The lovely seasonal Christmas rose makes a quick and an attractive motif to stitch.

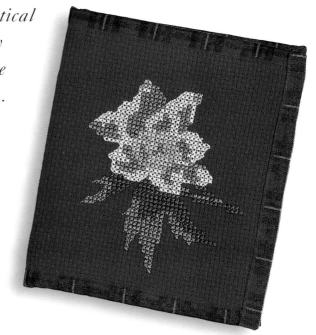

Measurements

The wallet measures 10 x 12cm (4¾ x 4in)

Materials

• Piece of red 14-count aida fabric measuring 24 x 18cm (9½ x 7in)

• Another piece of red aida fabric measuring 22 x 13cm (8¾ x 5⅛in)

• DMC or Anchor stranded embroidery cotton, one skein each of the colours shown in the chart

• Tapestry needle, size 24

• Piece of 1.5cm-(½in-)wide tartan ribbon 1m (39½in) in length

• Two pieces of iron-on bonding material, one measuring 12 x 20cm (4¾ x 8in) and the other 11 x 20cm (4½ x 8in)

To make up

Fold the larger piece of aida in half widthways and position the design so that it is 5cm (2in) down from the top. Work the design using three strands of embroidery thread. Each square represents one cross stitch. Where squares are shown divided diagonally, with half in one colour, half in another, work three-quarter and quarter cross stitches (see p.105).

Press the completed work on the reverse using a hot iron setting (see p.106), then make up the wallet following the instructions given on p.107.

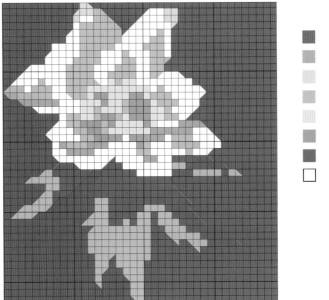

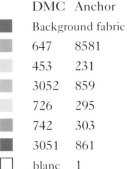

	DMC	Anchor
	Background fabric	
	647	8581
	453	231
	3052	859
	726	295
	742	303
	3051	861
	blanc	1

Rosehip Needlecase

Perhaps this stylish case should be the first item you make from this book, so that you can keep all your needles in it! Line it with gold fabric for a luxurious look.

To make up

To position the design, fold the aida in half lengthways and mark the middle point with a line of basting stitches. Work the design on the right-hand side, two aida squares from the centre fold-line. Make sure that you centre the design top and bottom. Following the chart, work the design in cross stitch using two strands of embroidery thread. Each square represents one cross stitch. Press the completed work on the reverse using a hot iron setting (see p.106), then make up the needlecase following the instructions that are given on p.107.

Measurements

The rosehip needlecase measures 9 x 8cm (3½ x 3⅛in)

Materials

• Piece of navy-blue 18-count aida fabric measuring 14 x 20.5cm (5½ x 8in)
• DMC or Anchor stranded embroidery cotton, one skein each of the colours in the chart
• Tapestry needle, size 26
• Piece of cardboard measuring 16 x 9cm (6¼ x 3½in)
• Piece of lining fabric measuring 18 x 11cm (7¼ x 4¼in)
• Two small pieces of felt measuring 14 x 8.5cm (5½ x 3⅜in)

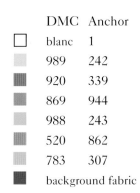

	DMC	Anchor
☐	blanc	1
	989	242
	920	339
	869	944
	988	243
	520	862
	783	307
	background fabric	

Glasses Case

A geometric pattern on a black background makes a striking design for this glasses case.
As the case can be used for spectacles or sunglasses, it can be stitched as a gift for anyone.

DMC	Anchor
	background fabric
3042	870
501	878
347	13
806	169

Measurements

The glasses case measures 11 x 18.5cm
(4¼ x 7¼in)

Materials

• Piece of black 14-count aida fabric measuring
38 x 24cm (15 x 9½in)
• DMC or Anchor stranded embroidery cotton,
one skein each of the colours shown in the chart
(below)
• Tapestry needle, size 24
• Two pieces of 1cm (½in) wadding (batting)
measuring 11 x 18cm (4¼ x 7in)
• Two pieces of red felt measuring 11 x 18cm
(4¼ x 7in)
• Twisted cord 75cm (29½in) in length

To make up

Cut the aida fabric into two pieces, each measuring 19 x 24cm (7½ x 9½in).

Following the chart and beginning centrally
(see p.104), work the design on one of the pieces
in cross stitch using two strands of embroidery
thread. Each square represents one cross stitch.
Work three designs across and six up.

Press the completed work on the reverse side
using a hot iron setting (see p.106), then make up
the glasses case following the instructions which
are given on p.107.

Sledging Pencil Case

Children will love to take this unusual pencil case to school. The embroidered panel is stitched to the velvet background and trimmed with twisted cord.

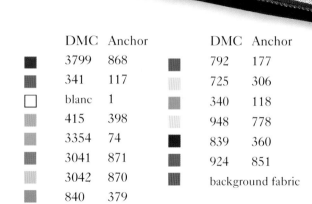

Measurements

The actual design measures 10 x 6 cm (4 x 2in).
The pencil case measures 20 x 13cm (8 x 5in)

Materials

• Piece of red 18-count aida fabric measuring 25 x 21cm (9¾ x 8¼in)
• Piece of red velvet or other fabric measuring 40 x 24cm (16 x 9¾in)
• DMC or Anchor stranded embroidery cotton, one skein each of the colours shown in the chart (below)
• Six small buttons
• Narrow twisted cord 47cm (18½ in) in length

	DMC	Anchor		DMC	Anchor
	3799	868		792	177
	341	117		725	306
	blanc	1		340	118
	415	398		948	778
	3354	74		839	360
	3041	871		924	851
	3042	870		background fabric	
	840	379			

To make up

Beginning centrally (see p.104), work the design on the aida in cross stitch using two strands of embroidery thread. Each square represents one cross stitch. Where squares are shown divided diagonally, with half in one colour, half in another, work three-quarter and quarter cross stitches (see p.105). When all the cross stitching is complete, outline the snow and the children's sleeves in gray back stitch using one strand of embroidery thread. Add the features in back stitch using one strand of thread in the colours shown in the chart.

Press the completed work on the reverse using a hot iron (see p.106), then make up the pencil case following the instructions given on p.108.

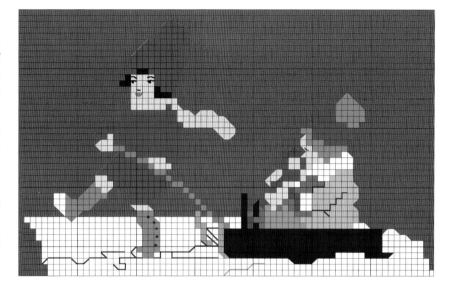

Cherub Brooch Pillow

A brooch cushion is a lovely way of displaying your collection and will be an unusual feature on a dressing table. Stars in metallic thread are stitched onto the velvet 'sky'.

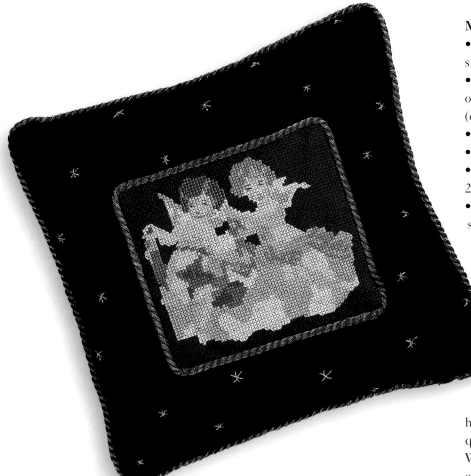

Materials
- Piece of dark-blue 18-count aida fabric measuring 24 x 23cm (9½ x 9in)
- DMC or Anchor stranded embroidery cotton, one skein each of the colours shown in the chart (opposite)
- Reel of DMC or Anchor silver thread
- Tapestry needle, size 26
- 2 pieces of dark-blue velvet measuring 21 x 22cm (8¼ x 9in)
- Length of narrow twisted cord or braid measuring 120cm (47in)
- Wadding for stuffing
- Pot pourri or lavender

To make up
Following the chart opposite and beginning centrally (see p.104), work the design in cross stitch using two strands of embroidery thread. Each square represents one cross stitch. Where squares are shown divided diagonally, with half in one colour and half in another, work three-quarter and quarter cross stitches (see p.105). When all the cross stitching is complete, add the cherubs' features in back stitch and straight stitches using one strand of embroidery thread in the colours shown in the chart.

Press the completed work on the reverse side using a hot iron setting (see p.106), and then make up the brooch pillow following the instructions given on p.108.

Measurements
The actual design measures 9.5 x 8cm (3¾ x 3¼in). The pillow measures 19 x 20cm (7½ x 8in)

DMC	Anchor	DMC	Anchor	DMC	Anchor	DMC	Anchor	DMC	Anchor
background fabric		415	398	948	778	309	42	320	215
3787	393	3045	888	950	4146	725	306	blanc	1
3046	887	598	167	335	41	807	168		

Robin's Box

This ornate little box can be given as a gift on its own, or used to enclose another present such as a brooch. Although it looks impressive, it does not take long to make.

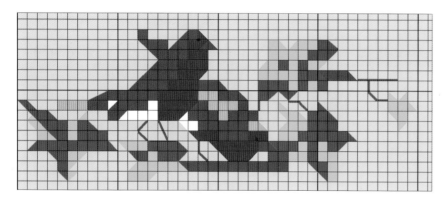

Measurements
The actual design measures 7.25 x 2.75cm (2⅞ x 1⅛in)

Materials
• Piece of light blue 14-count aida fabric measuring 22 x 17cm (8¾ x 6¾in)

• DMC or Anchor stranded embroidery cotton, one skein each of the colours shown in the chart
• Tapestry needle, size 24
• Box with lid measuring at least 7.25 x 5.5cm (2⅞ x 1⅛in)
• Length of ribbon to fit around all four sides of box lid
• Same length of ribbon to fit around sides of box
• Length of narrow twisted cord or braid to fit around box lid

To make up
Beginning centrally (see p.104), work the design in cross stitch using three strands of embroidery thread. Each square represents one cross stitch. Where squares are shown divided diagonally, with half in one colour, half in another, work three-quarter and quarter cross stitches (see p.105). When complete, work the robin's legs and the leaf stems in back stitch using two strands in the colours shown in the chart.

Press the completed work on the reverse using a hot iron setting (see p.106), then make up the box following the instructions given on p.108.

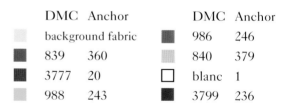

	DMC	Anchor			DMC	Anchor
	background fabric			▪	986	246
▪	839	360		▪	840	379
▪	3777	20		☐	blanc	1
▪	988	243		▪	3799	236

Snowball Fight Paperweight

A snowball fight is a seasonal subject for this useful gift. Worked on a fine-gauge fabric, the little scene has plenty of detail and is full of action.

Measurements
The actual design measures 6.5cm (2½in) square

Materials
• Piece of white 18-count aida fabric measuring 21cm (8¼in) square
• DMC or Anchor stranded embroidery cotton, one skein each of the colours shown in the chart (below)
• Tapestry needle, size 26
• Round glass paperweight measuring 8.75cm (3½in) in diameter

To make up
Following the chart and beginning centrally (see p.104), work the design in cross stitch using two strands of embroidery thread. Each square represents one cross stitch. Where squares are shown divided diagonally, with half in one colour and half in another, work three-quarter and quarter cross stitches (see p.105). When all the cross stitching is complete, outline some areas of snow in light gray back stitch using one strand of embroidery thread. Add the boys' features in back stitch and straight stitches using one strand of thread in the colours shown in the chart.

Press the completed work on the reverse side using a hot iron setting (see p.106), and then make up the paperweight following the instructions given on p.109.

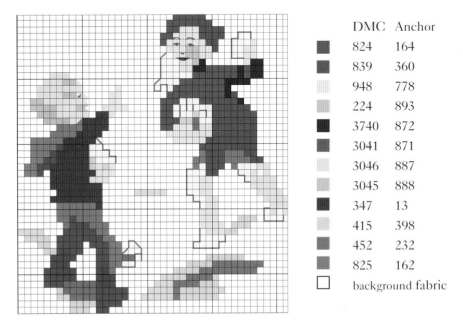

	DMC	Anchor
	824	164
	839	360
	948	778
	224	893
	3740	872
	3041	871
	3046	887
	3045	888
	347	13
	415	398
	452	232
	825	162
	background fabric	

Decorative Buttons

Hand-stitched buttons are a very unusual and effective present. They are simple to make and add interest to a plain garment. The colours can be adjusted to match the outfit.

Measurements
Each button measures 2cm (¾in) in diameter

Materials
For three buttons:
• Piece of red 22-count Hardanger fabric measuring 17cm (6¾in) square
• DMC or Anchor stranded embroidery cotton, one skein each of the colours shown in the chart (opposite)
• Tapestry needle, size 26
• Three 22mm (¾in) self-covering plastic buttons

To make up
Following the chart below and beginning the stitching centrally (see p.104), work the design in cross stitch using two strands of embroidery thread. Each square on the chart represents one complete cross stitch. Position each button design on your fabric, making sure that there is plenty of space around each one to fit round the back of the button.

When finished the stitching, press the completed piece of work on the reverse side using a hot iron setting (see p.106), and then make up the buttons following the instructions that are given on p.109.

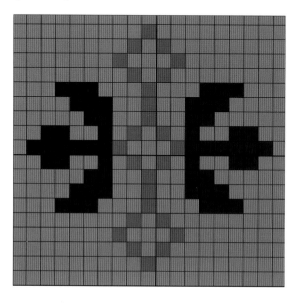

DMC	Anchor
background fabric	
791	178
890	683

Victorian Boy Brooch

Display your finest embroidery in this exquisite fob pin. The charming portrait of a young Victorian boy suits the style of the piece of jewellery perfectly.

Measurements
The actual design measures 2 x 2.5cm (¾ x 1in)

Materials
• Piece of cream 22-count Hardanger fabric measuring 12.5cm (5in) square
• DMC or Anchor stranded embroidery cotton, one skein each of the colours shown in the chart (opposite)
• Tapestry needle, size 26
• Fob brooch with oval frame measuring 3 x 4cm (1¼ x 1½in)

To make up
Following the chart on the right and beginning the stitching centrally (see p.104), work the design in cross stitch using one strand of embroidery thread. Each square on the chart represents one complete cross stitch. Where squares are shown divided diagonally, with half in one colour and half in another, work three-quarter and quarter cross stitches (see p.105). When all the cross stitching is complete, add the boy's features in fine back stitch and satin stitch, using a single strand of embroidery thread in the colours shown in the chart.

Press the completed work on the reverse using a hot iron setting (see p.106), then make up the brooch following the instructions given on p.109.

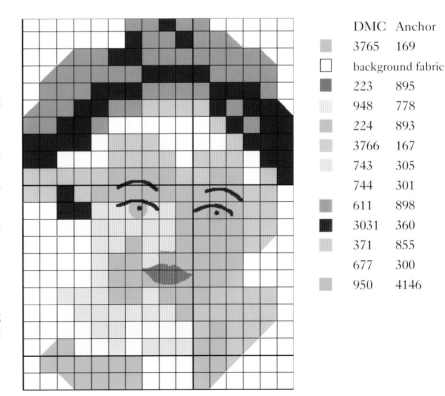

	DMC	Anchor
	3765	169
	background fabric	
	223	895
	948	778
	224	893
	3766	167
	743	305
	744	301
	611	898
	3031	360
	371	855
	677	300
	950	4146

Cherubs Cushion

A trio of appealing cherubs carry a garland and a wreath on the central panel of this beautiful cushion. The gentle colours will suit any decor.

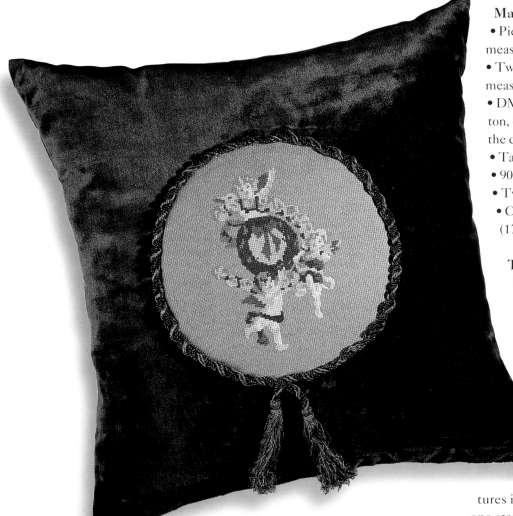

Materials
- Piece of gray-brown 16-count aida fabric measuring 28 cm (11in) square
- Two pieces of brown velvet or other fabric measuring 46 cm (18 in) square
- DMC or Anchor stranded embroidery cotton, one skein each of the colours shown in the chart (opposite)
- Tapestry needle, size 24
- 90cm (35½in) length of twisted cord
- Two tassels
- Cushion pad measuring 43cm (17in) square

To make up

Following the chart opposite and beginning the stitching centrally (see p.104), work the design in cross stitch using two strands of embroidery thread. Each complete square represents one cross stitch. Where squares are shown divided diagonally, with half in one colour and half in another, work three-quarter and quarter cross stitches (see p.105). When all the cross stitching is complete, add the cherubs' features in back stitch and straight stitches using one strand of embroidery thread in the colours shown in the chart.

Press the completed work on the reverse using a hot iron setting (see p.106), then make up the cushion following the instructions given on p.109.

Measurements
The cushion measures 43cm (17in) square. The central panel is 19cm (7½in) in diameter

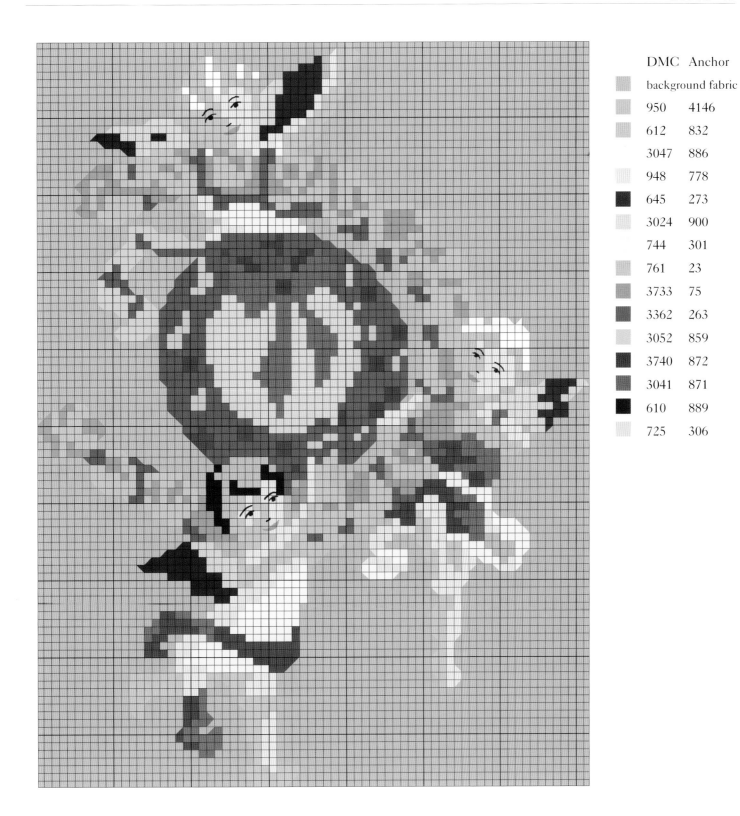

DMC	Anchor
background fabric	
950	4146
612	832
3047	886
948	778
645	273
3024	900
744	301
761	23
3733	75
3362	263
3052	859
3740	872
3041	871
610	889
725	306

Geometric Bookmark

This boldly patterned bookmark is simple to sew, as the design repeats itself along the length. You could make several in different colours.

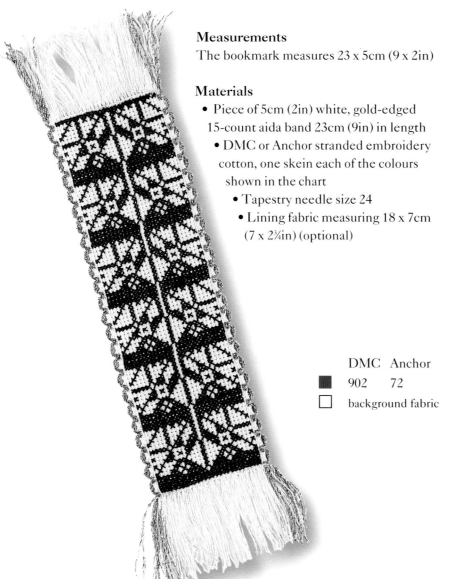

Measurements

The bookmark measures 23 x 5cm (9 x 2in)

Materials

- Piece of 5cm (2in) white, gold-edged 15-count aida band 23cm (9in) in length
- DMC or Anchor stranded embroidery cotton, one skein each of the colours shown in the chart
- Tapestry needle size 24
- Lining fabric measuring 18 x 7cm (7 x 2¾in) (optional)

To make up

Following the chart, work the design in cross stitch using two strands of embroidery thread. Each square represents one cross stitch. Start work 3.5cm (1⅜in) up from the lower edge of fabric to allow for the fringing. Work the design a total of six times; it should then measure 16cm (6¼in), leaving 3.5cm (1⅜in) of fabric for the fringing at the top.

Press the completed work on the reverse using a hot iron setting (see p.106), then make up the bookmark following the instructions that are given on p.109.

DMC	Anchor
902	72
background fabric	

Star and Berry Braid

These sparkling designs are simple to stitch, but make very eye-catching trimmings.

Measurements
The star braid is 2.5cm (1in) wide; the berry braid is 2.5cm (1in) wide

Materials
For the star braid, you will need:
• Length as required of 2.5cm (1in) cream 15-count aida band
• 1 reel of DMC or Anchor gold thread
• Tapestry needle, size 24

For the berry braid, you will need:
• Length as required of 2.5cm (1in) cream 15-count aida band
• DMC or Anchor stranded embroidery cotton, one skein each of the colours shown in the chart
• Tapestry needle, size 24

To make up
To make the star braid, follow the chart below, working the outline with straight stitch and filling in with cross stitch. Each square represents one cross stitch. Repeat the stars at 2.5cm/1in (16 squares) intervals until you achieve the required length. To make the berry, work the entire design in cross stitch, following the chart and using two strands of embroidery thread. Each square represents one cross stitch. Repeat the pattern until you achieve the required length.

Press the completed works on the reverse using a hot iron (see p.106), then turn under a double hem on the raw edges and slipstitch down.

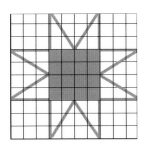

	DMC	Anchor
☐	background fabric	
▨	gold	gold

	DMC	Anchor
▨	500	879
▨	355	341
☐	background fabric	

Christmas Stocking

This is a good-sized stocking to hang at the end of the bed or from the mantelpiece. The design on the front panel is a foretaste of all the exciting gifts to come.

Measurements

The actual design measures 7.5 x 13.5cm (3 x 5¼in). The stocking is 40cm (15¾in) long and 17cm (6¾in) wide at the top

Materials

• Piece of black 14-count aida fabric measuring 18 x 26cm (7 x 10¼in)
• DMC or Anchor stranded embroidery cotton, one skein each of the colours shown in the chart (opposite)
• Tapestry needle, size 24
• Piece of black velvet fabric measuring 44 x 58cm (17½ x 23in)
• Piece of netting or lace measuring 38 x 22cm (15 x 8½in)
• 55cm (21½in) length of 0.6cm (¼in) ribbon

To make up

Beginning centrally (see p.104) and following the chart opposite, work the design in cross stitch using three strands of embroidery thread. Each square represents one cross stitch. Where squares are shown divided diagonally, with half in one colour and half in another, work three-quarter cross stitches (see p.105). When the stitching is complete, add the dog's and child's features in back stitch and satin stitch using two strands in the charted colours.

Press the work on the reverse using a hot iron setting (see p.106), then make up the stocking following the instructions given on p.109.

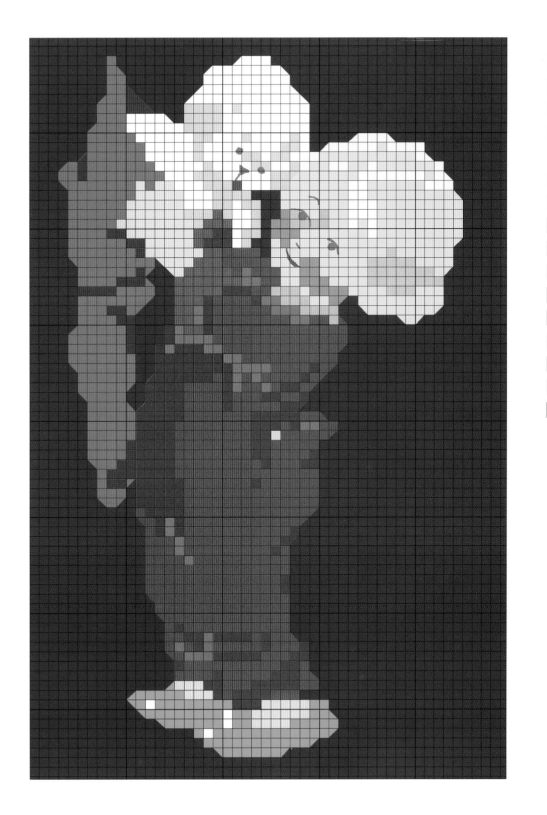

DMC	Anchor
background fabric	
825	162
824	164
415	398
3047	886
3046	887
948	778
3041	871
224	893
950	4146
815	22
347	13
3045	888
413	401
991	189
blanc	1

TABLE LINEN

Table Dressing

In many ways, Christmas is a particularly special time for children – for whom, of course, the main focus is on Santa Claus, snowmen, carol singing and Christmas trees. For many adults, the season's festivities retain their irresistible nostalgic charm but revolve largely around food and drink: Christmas dinner is often the unchallenged highpoint of the holiday. Meals at Christmas aren't really complete without special table settings. A beautifully laid table helps to create a festive atmosphere, and I'm sure that the three designs for table linen shown in this chapter will win you many compliments, while the bib design makes sure that even the youngest members of the family are not left out of the fun.

If you like bright colours, then the tartan design is the obvious one to choose. Extra depth is given to this design by varying the number of strands of embroidery thread used for different bands of colours: where only one strand is used, more of the background fabric shows through than where two are used. These cheery, bold primary colours will brighten up the grayest Christmas Day and put everyone in a festive mood at the table. There are patterns for table mats, napkins, napkin rings and a doily that you can use to line a basket of bread rolls, croissants, sweets or biscuits. The napkins and doily are made up in holly-green fabric for contrast, but they could just as well all be made in red if preferred. The tartan mats would look equally effective on an old polished wooden table, maybe with red candles in antique candle holders, on a modern table decorated with red crackers and a bright centrepiece, or placed with stylish simplicity on top of a crisp, white tablecloth.

The mistletoe table linen has much paler, subtler colours. There are two different mistletoe designs, a trailing border and a sprig. The sprig is used for the tablecloth, but the trailing border could be sewn around the edge instead if you prefer. The mistletoe border could also edge a tray cloth for a luxury breakfast in bed, or be stitched onto aida band to make a bookmark. The mistletoe set comprises a tablecloth, napkins, table mats, napkin rings and a cake border – just the thing to add the ideal finishing touch to your Christmas cake. It would look perfect arrayed on a table with a centrepiece of greenery, along with white candles set in silver or pewter candlesticks.

The table mats and napkin rings with the versatile goose motifs are made in a beautiful rich green, which complements the pale grays and white of the waddling birds. The napkins and bread basket liner which complete the set are made in cream fabric, and have a design of two intertwined geese. If you would like the whole set to match, you could make the table mats and napkin rings in cream fabric with the design of the two entwined geese, or alternatively, the whole set could be made in green. Either of the goose motifs would also make

delightful tree decorations or Christmas cards. As an alternative, they could be sewn onto the wallet from the Gifts chapter or made into a paperweight. Fine cream muslin would make a lovely filmy tablecloth to place under this set, as would an old lacy curtain. Dark green, gold or silver candles would complete the picture.

Mistletoe Table Linen

The distinctive foliage and pale colours of mistletoe look very delicate on this set of cream table linen. Use single sprigs or an undulating border design.

To make up

When you stitch the border, position it on the right-hand side of the fabric, 3.5cm (1⅜in) from the top and bottom edges, and 3.5cm (1⅜in) in from the right-hand edge.

Following the chart on p.86, work the design in cross stitch using two strands of embroidery thread. Each square represents one cross-stitch worked over two fabric threads each way.

When the embroidery is complete, press the whole piece of fabric on the reverse side using a hot iron setting (see p.106). To finish, turn under a double 1cm (⅜in) hem around all four sides of the table mat.

CAKE BORDER

Measurements
The cake border measures 5cm (2in) in width. The repeat pattern measures 10.5 x 4.25cm (4⅛ x 1⅝in) in length

Materials
• 15-count aida band, measuring 5cm (2in) in width, and the required length of your cake, plus 5cm (2in) for hems
• DMC or Anchor stranded embroidery cotton, one skein each of the colours shown in the chart (overpage)
• Tapestry needle, size 24
• Two press-stud fasteners

TABLE MAT

Measurements
The mistletoe table mat measures 47 x 33cm (18½ x 13in). The mistletoe border design measures 5cm (2in) across and 30cm (11¾in) from top to bottom

Materials
• Piece of cream 27-count evenweave fabric measuring 51 x 37cm (20 x 14½in)
• DMC or Anchor stranded embroidery cotton, one skein each of the colours shown in the chart
• Tapestry needle, size 26

To make up

To calculate the circumference of your cake wind a length of string or cord around the cake and add 5cm (2in) to this measurement for turnings.

When you stitch the mistletoe design, make sure to leave 2.5cm (1in) for the hem allowance. Following the chart below and beginning at one end of the aida band, work the design in cross stitch using two strands of embroidery thread. Each square represents one cross stitch. Repeat the design every two mistletoe sprigs until the border is the length for your cake.

Press the completed work on the reverse using a hot iron setting (see p.106). Finally, turn under a double 1.3cm (½in) hem at each end of the border and attach the press stud fasteners.

DMC	Anchor
☐ background fabric	
▨ 415	398
▨ 3363	262
▨ 3364	260

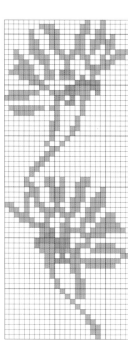

NAPKIN RING

Measurements
The napkin ring measures 27 x 5cm (10½ x 2in)

Materials
• Piece of 27-count cream evenweave fabric measuring 30 x 13cm (12 x 5in) for each napkin
• DMC or Anchor stranded embroidery cotton, one skein each of the colours shown in the chart (opposite page)
• Tapestry needle, size 26
• Cream tassel

To make up
When you stitch the design, position the top of the motif 7.25cm (2⅞in) down from the top of the fabric, the right-hand edge of the motif 6.5cm (2½in) in from the right-hand edge of the fabric and the bottom of the motif 2cm (¾in) up from the lower edge. Following the chart on p.87, work the design in cross stitch using two strands of embroidery thread. Each square represents one cross stitch worked over two fabric threads each way. Where squares are divided diagonally, half in one colour, half in another, work three-quarter cross stitches (see p.105). Work the stems in back stitch using one strand of embroidery thread in the charted colours.

When the embroidery is complete, press the finished work on the reverse using a hot iron setting (see p.106). To finish, fold the fabric in half lengthways, wrong sides together, and press. Fold the two top corners back to make a point. Slipstitch around the edges of the napkin ring and stitch the folded-back corners into place. Sew the tassel on to the point and attach the press stud fasteners to hold the pointed end of the napkin ring in place overlapping the other end.

To make up

When you come to stitch the mistletoe design, position it in the top right-hand corner of your piece of aida fabric so that the top of the motif is approximately 4cm (1½in) down from the top edge of the fabric, and the right-hand edge is about 4cm (1½in) in from the right-hand edge of the fabric.

Following the mistletoe pattern charted below, work the design in cross stitch, using two strands of embroidery thread. Each square represents one complete cross stitch worked over two threads of fabric each way. Where squares are shown on the chart as divided diagonally, with half picked out in one colour and half in another colour, work three-quarter cross stitches (see p.105). When all the cross stitching is finally completed, work the fine stems of the mistletoe pattern in back stitch, using one strand of embroidery thread in the colours that are shown in the chart.

Once your piece of embroidery is complete, turn the fabric over and press the finished work on the reverse side using a hot iron setting (see p.106). To finish the table napkin, turn under and neatly stitch a double 1cm (⅜in) hem around all the edges of the piece.

NAPKIN

Measurements

The napkin measures 39cm (15¼in) square. The motif measures 6 x 3.75cm (2¼ x 1½in)

Materials

• Piece of 27-count cream evenweave fabric measuring 43cm (17in) square for each napkin
• DMC or Anchor stranded embroidery cotton, one skein each of the colours shown in the chart (right)
• Tapestry needle, size 26

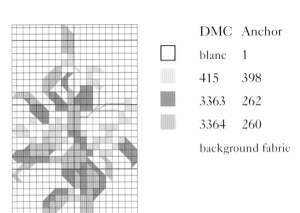

	DMC	Anchor
☐	blanc	1
	415	398
	3363	262
	3364	260
	background fabric	

TABLECLOTH

Measurements
The tablecloth measures 96cm (37¾in) square. Each mistletoe motif measures 6 x 3.75cm (2¼ x 1½in)

Materials
• Piece of cream 27-count evenweave fabric measuring 102cm (40in) square, or to fit your table
• DMC or Anchor stranded embroidery cotton in the colours shown in the chart on previous page: one skein each of 415/398, blanc/1; two skeins each of 3363/262, 3364/260
• Tapestry needle, size 26

To make up
Before you begin, turn under a double 1.5cm (½in) hem all around the fabric to prevent fraying.

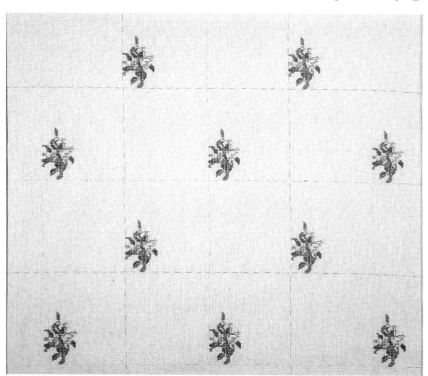

Fold the fabric into four to find the middle and run rows of basting stitches along the horizontal and vertical creases, crossing at the centre point.

Following the chart on p.87, work the first mistletoe motif centred on the crossed lines of basting stitches, using two strands of embroidery thread. Each square represents one cross stitch worked over two fabric threads each way. Where squares are shown divided diagonally, with half in one colour and half in another, work three-quarter cross stitches (see p.105). When all the cross stitching is complete, work the fine stems in back stitch using one strand of embroidery thread in the colours shown in the chart.

Next, add two more lines of basting stiches, one on either side of the horizontal line and 19cm (7½in) from it. Stitch two more mistletoe motifs centred on the points where these new lines of basting stitches cross the centre vertical. You should now have a vertical row of three stitched motifs. Stitch two lines of basting stitches parallel to the centre vertical and 21.5cm (8½in) from it. Work two rows of mistletoe motifs centred on the crossing points of these lines to match up exactly with the first row.

Now position the rows of motifs that fall in between the rows already worked and which are staggered with the previous ones. Run two lines of basting stitches on either side of the centre vertical and 10.5cm (4¼in) from it, and two more lines of basting 21.5cm (8½in) to the left and right of these. Next, run two lines of basting on either side of the centre horizontal and 9cm (3½in) from it, and two more lines of basting 19cm (7½in) above and below these. Stitch sixteen mistletoe motifs centred on each of the crossing points.

When all the cross stitching is complete, remove the basting threads. Finally, press the completed work on the reverse using a hot iron setting (see p.106).

Christmas Pudding Cake Border

*Make your Christmas cake even more
appetizing with this festive border.*

Measurements
The design measures 10.5 x 4.5cm (4¼ x 1¾in).

Materials
• 15-count, gold-edged aida band, measuring
5cm (2in) in width, and the required length of
your cake, plus 5cm (2in) for hems
• DMC or Anchor stranded embroidery cotton,
one skein each of the colours shown in the chart
• Tapestry needle, size 24
• Two hook-and-eye fasteners

To make up
First, work out how many designs will fit along
your band. A border 52.5cm (20¾in) long will fit
around a cake 15cm (6in) in diameter. To make a
border this size, divide the band with vertical
rows of basting stitches starting 2cm (¾in) from one
edge. Make a second row of stitches 3cm (1¼in)
from the first, and a third 10.5cm (4¼in) from the
second. The first pattern repeat will fit into this
space. Leave a 5cm (2in) space, then repeat the
lines at 10.5cm (4¼in) and 5cm (2in) intervals.
Following the chart, work the repeat patterns in
the spaces. Work in cross stitch using two strands
of thread. Each square represents one cross stitch.
Next, add the features in back stitch using one
strand of thread. Finally, press the completed
work, turn under a double 1cm (⅜in) hem at either
end of the band and attach the fasteners.

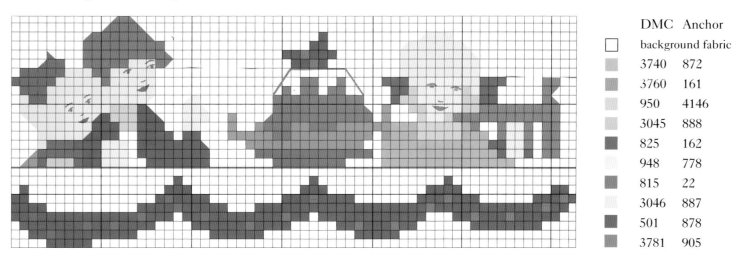

DMC	Anchor
background fabric	
3740	872
3760	161
950	4146
3045	888
825	162
948	778
815	22
3046	887
501	878
3781	905

Goose Table Linen

Two different designs featuring geese, a single bird and a goose and gander in a pair, are fun to stitch on to a set of table linen for the breakfast or tea table at Christmas time.

TABLE MAT

Measurements
The table mat measures 52 x 38cm (20½ x 15in). The motif measures 4 x 3.5cm (1½ x 1⅜in)

Materials
• Piece of green 22-count Hardanger fabric measuring 52 x 38cm (21½ x 15in) for each table mat
• DMC or Anchor stranded embroidery cotton, one skein each of the colours shown in the chart
• Tapestry needle, size 26

To make up
Following the chart right, work the first goose 2.5cm (1in) down from the top of the piece of fabric. The outer edge of the goose on the right should be 4.5cm (1¾in) in from the right-hand side of the fabric. Work in cross stitch using one strand of embroidery thread. Each square represents one cross-stitch. Where squares are shown divided diagonally, with half in one colour and half in another, work three-quarter cross stitches (see p.105). Position the rest of the geese along

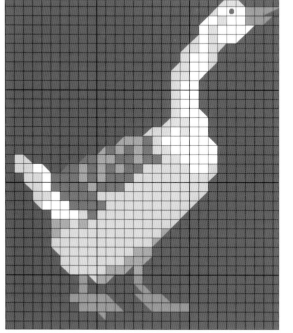

	DMC	Anchor
☐	blanc	1
▨	413	401
▨	317	400
▨	977	313
▨	415	398
▨	background fabric	

the right-hand edge of the mat at 3cm (1¼in) intervals. When all the cross stitching is complete, add the geese's eyes with tiny straight

stitches using one strand of embroidery thread in the colour shown in the chart.

When the embroidery is complete, make up the table mat as follows. Pull out a thread on all four sides of the fabric, 1.5cm (½in) from the edge. Using matching thread, sew a line of machine zigzag stitch just inside the gap created by the pulled thread, to prevent it from unravelling. Next, remove the threads outside the zigzag line to form a fringe. Finally, press the completed work on the reverse side using a hot iron setting (see p.106).

NAPKIN RING

Measurements
The napkin ring measures 19 x 6.5cm (7½ x 2½in). The motif measures 4 x 3.5cm (1½ x 1⅜in)

Materials
- Piece of green 22-count Hardanger fabric measuring 21 x 15cm (8¼ x 6in) for each napkin ring
- DMC or Anchor stranded embroidery cotton, one skein each of the colours shown in the chart
- Tapestry needle, size 26
- Two press stud fasteners

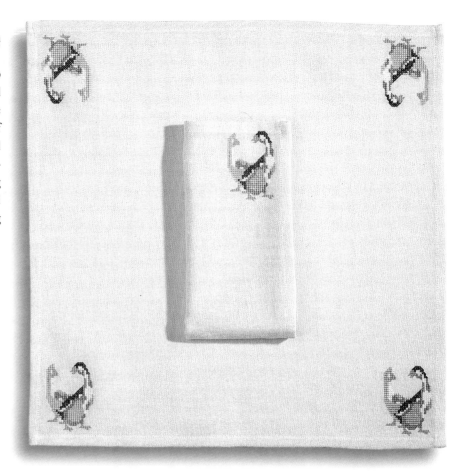

To make up
When you stitch the motif, position it 8.5cm (3⅜in) down from the top of the fabric, 2.5cm (1in) up from the lower edge of the fabric and 8.75cm (3½in) in from each side.

Following the chart on p.90, work the design in cross stitch using one strand of thread. Each square represents one cross stitch.

Where squares are shown divided diagonally, with half in one colour and half in another, work three-quarter cross stitches (see p.105). When all the cross stitching is complete, work the eye with a tiny straight stitch using one strand of thread.

When the embroidery is complete, press under a 1cm (⅜in) hem all around, fold the fabric in half lengthways, wrong sides facing, and press. Slipstitch around the edges of the napkin ring and sew on the press stud fasteners.

NAPKIN

Measurements
The napkin measures 39cm (15¼in) square. The motif measures 6.5 x 4.5cm (2½ x 1¾in).

Materials
• Piece of cream 27-count evenweave fabric measuring 43cm (17in) square
• DMC or Anchor stranded embroidery cotton, one skein each of the colours shown in the chart
• Tapestry needle, size 26

To make up
When you stitch the design, position it in the top right-hand corner of the fabric so that the top of the motif is 3cm (1¼in) down from the top edge of the fabric, and the right-hand edge is 3cm (1¼in) in from the right-hand edge of the fabric.

Following the chart right, work the design in cross stitch using two strands of embroidery thread. Each square represents one cross stitch worked over two fabric threads. Where squares are shown divided diagonally, with half in one colour and half in another colour, work three-quarter cross stitches (see p.105).

When the embroidery is complete, press on the reverse using a hot iron setting (see p.106). To finish, turn under a double 1cm (⅜in) hem around all four edges of the napkin.

BREAD BASKET LINER

Measurements
The basket liner measures 39cm (15¼in) square. The motif measures 6.5 x 4.5cm (21/2 x 13/4in).

Materials
• Piece of cream 27-count evenweave fabric measuring 43cm (17in) square
• DMC or Anchor stranded embroidery cotton, one skein each of the colours shown in the chart
• Tapestry needle, size 26

To make up
When you stitch the bread basket liner, position

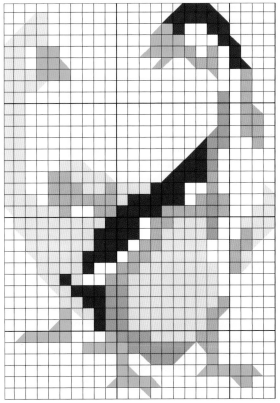

DMC	Anchor
blanc	1
3045	888
451	233
977	313
415	398
413	401

background fabric

the four geese motifs so that two of them have their feet toward the top of the fabric and the other two have their feet toward the bottom of the fabric. In each case, the motifs should be 3cm (1⅛in) in from each edge of the corner. Following the chart above, work the designs in cross stitch using two strands of embroidery thread. Each square represents one cross stitch over two fabric threads each way. Where squares on the chart are shown divided diagonally, with half in one colour and half in another, work three-quarter cross stitches (see p.105).

When your piece of embroidery is complete, press the whole work on the reverse side using a hot iron setting (see p.106). To finish, turn under a double 1cm (⅜in) hem around all four edges of the fabric.

Tartan Table Linen

For those of you who like colourful linen, here is a set in rich, Christmas shades. You can give extra depth to the design by varying the number of strands of embroidery thread used for different bands of colour.

To make up

When you come to stitch the design, position the motif approximately 3cm (1⅛in) in from the right-hand side of the piece of fabric and about 3.5cm (1⅜in) in from the top and bottom edges of the fabric.

Following the chart below, work the design in cross stitch. Each square on the chart represents one complete cross stitch. Use two strands of embroidery thread for the charted yellow, white, gray and the darker shades of the two blues and greens, and use a single strand of embroidery thread for the lighter of the two blues and greens.

TABLE MAT

Measurements

The table mat overall measures 43 x 30cm (17 x 12in). The tartan motif itself measures 3.5 x 28.2cm (1⅜ x 11⅛in).

Materials

• Piece of red 14-count aida fabric measuring 47 x 34cm (18½ x 13½in)
• DMC or Anchor stranded embroidery cotton, one skein each of the colours shown in the chart
• Tapestry needle, size 24

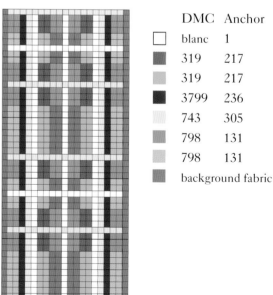

	DMC	Anchor
	blanc	1
	319	217
	319	217
	3799	236
	743	305
	798	131
	798	131
	background fabric	

(This is to allow more red to show through from the base fabric and thus make it look more like real tartan.)

When the embroidery is finished, turn it over and press the completed work on the reverse using a hot iron setting (see p.106). To finish, turn under and stitch a double 1cm (⅜in) hem all round the mat.

NAPKIN RING

Measurements

The ring measures 26 x 6cm (10¼ x 2¼in). The motif measures 4.25 x 3.75cm (1⅝ x 1½in).

Materials

• Piece of red 14-count aida fabric measuring 29 x 15cm (11½ x 6in) for each napkin ring
• DMC or Anchor stranded embroidery cotton, one skein each of the colours shown in the chart
• Tapestry needle, size 24
• Two press stud fasteners

To make up

When you are stitching the design, position the motif 8cm (3⅛in) down from the top of the fabric, 4.5cm (1¾in) in from the right-hand edge, 2cm (¾in) up from the lower edge and 18cm (7in) in from the left-hand edge. Following the chart left, work the design in cross stitch. Each square represents one cross stitch. Use two strands of embroidery thread for the yellow, white, gray and the darker blue and green on the chart; use one strand for the light blue and green.

Once the embroidery is completed, press the finished work on the reverse side using a hot iron setting (see p.106), then make up the napkin ring as follows. Press under a 1.5cm (½in) turning on all sides, fold the fabric in half lengthways with wrong sides together, and press. Fold the two top corners to the back to make a point. Slipstitch around the edges of the napkin ring and stitch the folded-back corners in position. Sew a tassel on to the pointed end of the napkin ring and attach the press stud fasteners to hold the pointed end in place overlapping the other end.

DMC	Anchor
blanc	1
319	217
319	217
3799	236
798	131
798	131
743	305
background fabric	

NAPKIN

Measurements

The napkin measures 39cm (15¼in) square. The motif measures 4.25 x 4.25cm (1⅝ x 1⅝in).

Materials

• Piece of dark green 22-count Hardanger fabric measuring 43cm (17 in) square
• DMC or Anchor stranded embroidery cotton, one skein each of the colours shown in the chart
• Tapestry needle, size 26

To make up

When you are stitching the design, position the motif 4cm (1½in) in from each side of a corner. Following the chart opposite, work the design in cross stitch. Each square represents one cross stitch worked over two threads of Hardanger fabric each way. Use two strands of embroidery thread for the white, yellow, dark gray and the darker red and blue on the chart; use one strand of embroidery thread for the light blue and red.

When the embroidery is complete, press the completed work on the reverse using a hot iron setting (see p.106). To finish, turn under a double 1cm (⅜in) hem all around the napkin.

BREAD BASKET LINER

Measurements

The basket liner measures 39cm (15¼in) square. The design measures 4.25 x 4.25 cm (1⅝ x 1⅝in).

Materials

• Piece of dark green 22-count Hardanger fabric measuring 43 x 43cm (17 x 17in)
• DMC or Anchor stranded embroidery cotton, one skein each of the colours shown in the chart
• Tapestry needle, size 26

To make up

When you are stitching the design, position each of the four squares of tartan 4cm (1½in) in from each side of a corner. Following the chart opposite, work the design in cross stitch. Each square represents one cross stitch worked over two threads of Hardanger fabric each way. Use two strands of embroidery thread for the yellow, dark gray, white, darker red and darker blue on the chart; use one strand for the paler red and blue.

When the embroidery is complete, press the completed work on the reverse using a hot iron setting (see p.106). To finish, turn under a double 1cm (⅜in) hem all round the edge of the doily.

Rabbit Bib

This rabbit carrying a mistletoe sprig and some presents will add a festive note to baby's Christmas. The design is worked over waste canvas, so it can be stitched on to any fabric.

Measurements

The actual design measures 7 x 11cm (2¾ x 4¼in). The bib illustrated measures overall 16.5 x 21.5cm (6½ x 8½in)

Materials

• Piece of 12-count waste canvas measuring 10 x 12cm (4 x 4¾in)
• DMC or Anchor stranded embroidery cotton, one skein each of the colours shown in the chart
• White towelling bib
• 56cm (22in) length of bottle green 0.6cm (¼in) ribbon, or length required to go around the edge of the bib

To make up

Baste the waste canvas to the bib, making sure that it is straight and centred. Following the chart opposite and beginning centrally (see p.104), work the design in cross stitch using two strands of thread. Each square represents one cross stitch. Where squares are shown divided diagonally, with half in one colour and half in another, work three-quarter cross stitches (see p.105). Next, work the mistletoe stem and the balloon's string in back stitch using two strands of thread, and add the rabbit's features in back stitch and satin stitch.

When the cross stitching is complete, moisten the waste canvas and pull it out from underneath the embroidery thread by thread. A pair of tweezers is useful for this. Sew ribbon around the edge of the bib, turning under the ends neatly.

DMC	Anchor
840	379
797	132
839	360
796	133
561	212
3072	274
676	891
3721	896
3722	895
677	300
3041	871
221	897
3740	872
3371	382
	background fabric

TECHNIQUES & MATERIALS

Materials and Equipment

Fabrics

To form the perfectly square stitches necessary for a cross-stitch design, you will need to use evenweave fabric. Evenweave means that the fabric has the same number of horizontal (weft) threads and vertical (warp) threads over a given measurement.

Aida is the most suitable fabric for beginners to work on, as it is woven to form little squares over which each cross stitch is worked. It comes in a good range of colours, several of which I have used in this book. Easy-count aida is especially helpful for inexperienced stitchers as it is woven with a removable grid of contrasting threads every 10 squares – the same as the grid on most charts. However, it is more expensive than ordinary aida fabric and is usually only available in white and cream.

When the "count" of a fabric is specified in a design, this means the number of square blocks per 2.5cm (1in) in aida fabric, or the number of threads per 2.5cm (1in) in ordinary evenweave fabric. The higher the count, the smaller the completed item will be.

Aida fabric ranges from 6-count (the binca of primary school days!) to 18-count; the projects in this book are worked on 14-, 16- and 18-count aida. Aida band has also been used in the book, and comes in white with different coloured edgings, and in cream with a cream edging. It is a 15-count fabric and is available in three widths: 2.5cm (1in), 5cm (2in) and 10cm (4in).

Another kind of evenweave fabric useful for very fine cross-stitch work is Hardanger, a 22-count fabric which is woven with pairs of threads and is available in many colours. In addition, there is a wide range of single-thread evenweave fabrics, both natural and synthetic, some with as many as 36 threads to 2.5cm (1in). On single-thread evenweave fabric, cross stitches are worked over two threads each way. Thus a cross-stitch design worked on 36-count linen and on 18-count aida would come up the same size. For all these embroidery fabrics, you can buy ready-cut pieces for smaller projects if you wish.

Waste canvas is a very useful material that allows cross stitch to be worked on any fabric on which the threads cannot be easily counted. You can therefore use cross-stitch designs on pillowcases, aprons, children's clothes and other such items. Waste canvas comes in a range of mesh sizes from 8 to 14 and is 68cm (27in) wide. To use waste canvas, baste it where you intend to stitch, aligning the weave of the waste canvas to the weave of the fabric. Then, using the waste canvas as a guide for stitching, sew the cross stitch through both the canvas and the fabric together. When the design is completed, moisten the canvas, then carefully pull out all the horizontal threads of the waste canvas, one at a time. Follow this by pulling out all the vertical threads, then rinse the project thoroughly so that any waste canvas starch is removed from the fabric.

Threads

The thread used in this book is DMC stranded cotton, which is available in an enormous range of colours. The equivalent shade numbers in Anchor stranded cotton are also given with each design. Stranded cotton, also called embroidery floss, is made up of six strands which can be separated and recombined to make up the number you require. It is double mercerized, which gives it a silky texture, and is colourfast.

Previous pages: work in progress - what could be a more inspiring sight than an array of luscious-coloured threads, a tempting selection of embroidery fabrics ready to be worked, decorative tassels, a range of card mounts, and a piece of work – the Father Christmas card featured on p.20 – already underway.

A useful, although not essential, stitching accessory is a thread organizer. This comprises a thread-measuring card, a thread list and a project card. The measuring card allows you to cut all your threads to the desired length. You then fasten them by looping them onto the project card and you can write the colour numbers beside them. Thus, all the colours for one project are organized together, and there is usually a magnet at the top of the card to keep your needle safe.

Needles

Tapestry needles are used for all the projects in this book because their blunt points will not split the fibres of the fabric. A needle needs to be large enough to be easily threaded with the cotton required, but should be able to pass through the fabric without tugging.

The needle size for each design is specified in the project, but if you wish to adapt these or work your own designs, here is a rough guide to appropriate needle sizes: use a size 22 needle for 10- or 11-count fabric, a size 24 needle for 14- to 16-count fabric, and a size 26 needle for 18-, 22- and 25-count fabric. A larger needle, i.e. an 18, can be used for 10- or 11-count fabric if preferred.

Ring or hoop frames

You may prefer to work cross stitch without using a frame. Aida fabric is heavily sized so it should retain its shape if you stitch with an even tension, especially as cross stitch pulls the work in opposite directions all the time. However, I find that an embroidery hoop is much easier to use and gives better results. The "scooping" method used when the fabric is hand-held tends to distort the weave, whereas with a frame you work the stitches with a vertical "stabbing" motion, which distorts the fabric threads less and produces more even stitches. Stitching with one hand above and one below the work also speeds up the stitching.

Embroidery hoops are available in many sizes, and some clamp onto a table or floor stand, leaving both hands free for stitching. The fabric is stretched over the inner ring, and the outer ring holds it in place, tightened and secured by a screw.

When you have finished work for the day, take the fabric off the hoop, as the pressure of the rings can distort any stitches trapped between them and give uneven surface texture. Repositioning the hoop from time to time will help to prevent this. As marks can appear when dirt from the skin builds up on the fabric around the edges of the hoop, it is best to wash your hands each time you start work. Roll or wrap the work in acid-free tissue paper, or a clean white cloth such as muslin, at the end of each stitching session; rolling is better than folding as creases can be difficult to remove.

Scissors

Two pairs of scissors are needed for cross-stitch work – a sharp-pointed pair for cutting threads and a larger pair for cutting the fabric.

An embroidery hoop will keep the fabric taut while stitching. Rings or hoops come in wood or metal; floor stands are also available.

Before You Begin

Preparing fabrics for stitching

Make sure that you allow ample margins around the area of the embroidery when you cut out your fabric. A good margin for the smaller cross-stitch projects such as the cards and gift tags is 5cm (2in) all around, and for the larger ones 7.5cm (3in) all around. The margins are allowed for in the fabric requirements for the designs. For the gifts and the table linen, more precise measurements have been given to help you with positioning the motifs. In these cases, you could mark out the exact measurements on a larger piece of fabric with basting stitches or a washable marker. If you wish to work the embroidery in a hoop or frame of a particular size, you may need to increase the fabric margins slightly.

To prevent the raw edges of the fabric from fraying, sew around them with a machine zigzag stitch or oversew by hand. Alternatively, bind the edges with masking tape.

Marking the centre

Fold the fabric in half each way and crease lightly. Mark the crease lines with basting stitches, using sewing thread in a contrasting colour. An indelible or washable marker can be used, but if an indelible one is used, make sure that it does not show through the completed design. Do not use a pencil, because it will rub off onto the threads, and prove difficult to remove.

Where the two lines cross is the centre of the fabric. Find the middle of the chart to correspond; do this by counting out half the squares along the width and the height of the chart and marking the central points in pencil with arrows. Follow the arrows across the chart and where these lines cross mark the centre.

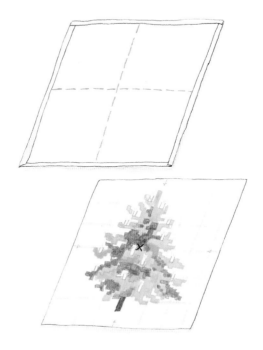

Before commencing work, mark the centre of the fabric by stitching two lines of basting stitches (top) in the form of a cross. The point where the two lines meet corresponds to the centre of the embroidered design on the grid chart (below). As a general rule, start working outwards from this central point.

Following a chart

Each square which shows part of the actual embroidered design on the grid of the chart represents one cross stitch, which is worked over one square of aida or Hardanger fabric, or over two threads of evenweave linen. The key gives you the thread number for each colour on the chart, in both DMC and Anchor shades. The other squares represent the background fabric.

For most of the designs, such as the cards and the pictures, the easiest way to begin is to work from the middle of the chart onto the corresponding centre of the fabric, stitching outward from here. With some of the gifts and table linen, where exact positioning instructions have been given, it is best to start stitching at one of the corners of the design.

Working the Stitches

Cross stitch

The cross consists of two diagonal stitches, one on top of the other. When working cross stitch, it is very important that you make sure that all the top stitches slant in the same direction, otherwise the embroidery will look untidy. Rows of cross stitch can be worked horizontally, vertically or diagonally. When stitching horizontally, it is economical with thread to work a row of the bottom stitches in one direction first, then cross them on the way back. When working vertically or diagonally you may find it easier to cross the stitches as you go along.

Work with about 45cm (18in) of stranded cotton in your needle. Separate all six strands, then recombine the number of threads required. This makes the coverage better. To begin stitching, bring the needle from the back to the front of the fabric, leaving a short end of thread measuring about 2cm (¾in) at the back. Secure this by working the first few stitches over it. Make sure that it is firm before continuing. Do not use a knot, as the lump will show.

When carrying a coloured thread from one part of the design to another, do not take it across the back of the fabric for more than 1.3cm (½in). Run it under previously worked stitches whenever possible. Fasten off the thread by running the needle under about five stitches at the back of the work and cutting the end off carefully.

Three-quarter and quarter stitches

Where squares are shown on the chart divided diagonally with half in one colour and half in another, this indicates three-quarter and quarter stitches. When a divided square is used on the outside edge of a charted design, work a three-quarter cross stitch. This consists of one diagonal stitch following the diagonal line in the square on the chart, and a quarter stitch meeting the diagonal in the middle of the square. Where a divided square is inside the design, stitch one part as a three-quarter and the other as a quarter stitch.

Stitches for details

Back stitch is used for outlining some parts of a design. Usually worked with one strand of thread in the needle, it creates a fine line which adds definition. I also use back stitch for facial features such as eyebrows, or, if only a tiny line is required, I use a straight stitch. Some features such as lips and the iris of an eye are filled in with satin stitch. Begin at the centre of a shape to establish the slant of the stitches, then work out to the sides. You may prefer to use a crewel needle, which has a sharp point, to work these details.

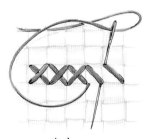

cross stitch

three-quarter stitch

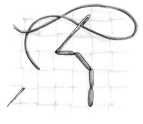

back stitch

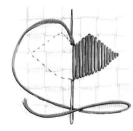

satin stitch

There are three basic stitches you need to master for cross-stitch work: cross stitch, three-quarter stitch and back stitch. Satin stitch is useful for filling in small areas, such as facial features.

Making-up Instructions

FINISHING THE EMBROIDERIES

Washing and pressing

It is not advisable to wash your cloth before you start stitching. However, you can wash your finished embroidery, providing you launder it in cool water using gentle soap flakes. Avoid rubbing the surface as this may damage the embroidery. Rinse thoroughly in cool water, but do not wring. Instead, roll the embroidery in a clean towel to absorb excess water. Unroll, right side down, onto a dry cloth, cover with lightweight fabric and press using a "cotton" iron setting until dry.

Before making up, it is important that you press your work. To do this, place the embroidery face down on a cotton sheet and press flat with a steam iron using a "cotton" setting.

MAKING UP THE PROJECTS

How to mount a card or gift tag

Lay the card or tag face down on a table and open out both flaps. Centre your embroidery over the aperture, then mark the fabric just inside the two folds of the card. Trim the embroidery so that it fits neatly inside the central panel.

Remove the embroidery, open out the flaps and cover the inside of the middle panel with glue or double-sided adhesive tape. Centre the aperture over the embroidery and press together. Finally, spread glue or tape over the inside surface of the left front panel of the card and fold it down onto the back of the design.

How to mount a picture

Cut a piece of acid-free backing board to fit your frame. Place this over the reverse side of your embroidery, and secure with masking tape along two opposite sides. Using strong thread and herringbone stitch, lace the excess fabric across the back of the boards, as shown. Begin at the middle of one side and work out to the corner. Pull the stitches taut. Lace the side edges in the same way, tucking the corners under neatly, then mount in a frame.

How to make a tree bauble

Place the embroidery right side up, then position a piece of tracing paper on top. Trace around the outside edge of the design with a pencil. Remove the tracing paper and cut out the shape. Place the paper template on a piece of felt and draw around it with a pen. Cut out the shape, adding 2mm (⅟₁₆in) all around. Cut out a piece of 2.5-cm (1-in) thick wadding to the same dimensions.

Cut out the embroidery design, adding a 2.5cm (1in) margin all around. Position the wadding on the wrong side. Fold the excess fabric back over the wadding and lace together. Place the piece of felt over the back and, using matching thread, oversew all around the edge. Leave a small hole at the bottom into which to push the ends of the braid. Push one end of the braid into the hole, then secure it around the front edges using small oversewing stitches. Create a loop at the top of the bauble and stitch the ends together. At the starting point, cut off the braid, leaving a 2cm (¾in) overlap. Push the end into the hole and stitch in place. Complete the decoration by oversewing the braid at the back.

How to make a tree sack

Trim the finished embroidery to 1cm (⅜in) all around. Fold under the raw edges and press.

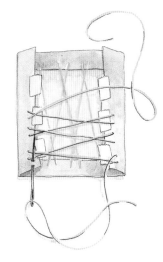

Mounting a picture, lacing the excess fabric over the back of the board. As you lace, keep checking that the right side of the fabric is being pulled evenly.

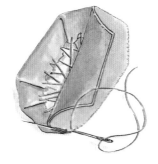

Making a tree bauble, sewing the felt backing into position.

Fold the fabric for the tree bag in half widthways, wrong sides together. Position the design so that it is 1cm (⅜in) up from the bottom edge and centred between each side. Oversew into position. With right sides together, fold the bag in half and and stitch along the sides taking a 1.5cm (½in) seam allowance. Turn under a small double hem along the top and stitch. Turn the bag right side out. Decorate the bottom with beads or fringing, sew on a hanging loop and finish with ribbon.

How to make a tree stocking

Cut out two stocking shapes, measuring 15cm (6in) in height, 12cm (4¾in) across the bottom and 9cm (3½in) across the top opening.

Fold under a 1cm (½in) hem around all edges of the embroidery and position the design toward the top half of one stocking. Baste, then oversew in place and finish with braid.

With right sides together, stitch the two stocking shapes together, leaving the top open. To finish, turn under a 1cm (½in) hem at the top opening.

How to make a wallet

Turn under 2cm (¾in) at each side of the embroidery and 3cm (¼in) at the top and bottom, press. Open out the larger piece of bonding material and position it centrally on the wrong side of the embroidery. Fold the edges of the aida back over the bonding material. On the smaller piece of aida, turn under 1cm (⅜in) all around the edge and press to form creases. Open out and iron on the bonding material centrally as before. Fold the edges of the aida back over the bonding material.

Bind the top edge of the inside pocket of the wallet with tartan ribbon. Place the two pieces of the wallet wrong sides together with the lower edges in line. Oversew together around three sides, leaving the top edge open. Bind the edges of the wallet with tartan ribbon, mitring the corners to fit neatly, and slipstitch in place.

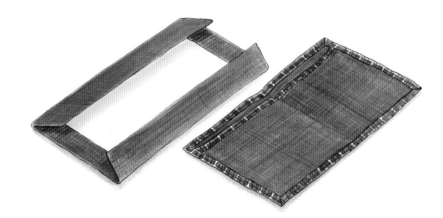

How to make a needlecase

Fold the cardboard in half widthways. Place the aida face down on a flat surface and put the cardboard centrally on top, lining up the two centre foldlines. Fold the sides of the aida back over the cardboard and press. Press the edges of the lining fabric under so that it is just slightly smaller than the needlecase to make sure that it doesn't show. Slipstitch the lining to the aida making sure that the needlecase closes properly. Place the two pieces of felt together centrally on the inside of the needlecase and attach to the central fold with a backstitch seam.

How to make a glasses case

Place the two pieces of felt together and stitch around three sides, leaving the top open. Attach a piece of wadding to each side and stitch in place.

Turn under the edges of the embroidery, six squares up from the top of the design, seven

Making a wallet, the bonding material ironed in position on the reverse side of the embroidery (top left). Finish the sewn wallet by binding the edges with tartan ribbon (top right).

Making a needlecase, attaching two pieces of felt to the central fold of the case with a backstitch seam (left).

squares down from the bottom of the design and three squares in from the outer edges. Trim the excess fabric to 1.5cm (½in) and press the turnings. Repeat this process with the other piece of aida so that they are both the same size.

Place a piece of aida on either side of the felt and wadding, with right sides out and the open end at the top. Oversew together around three sides, leaving the top open. Slipstitch the felt to the aida around the opening. Finish by sewing twisted cord around the top and side edges.

How to make a brooch pillow

Trim the aida to 12cm (4 ¾in) wide and 11cm (4¼in) high with an even amount of unworked fabric around the design. Turn under 1cm (⅜in) around all four edges and press. Pin and then slipstitch the embroidered panel onto the middle of one of the pieces of velvet, leaving a small gap into which to tuck the ends of the twisted cord. Push one end of the cord into the hole and slipstitch it around the edge of the panel. When you reach the starting point again, cut the cord with a 2cm (¾in) overlap and poke the end into the gap. Stitch up the gap, arranging the trimming so that it looks as if it continues unbroken around the edge. With silver thread, sew tiny stars all over the velvet with three crossing straight stitches tied down in the middle by a smaller stitch.

Place the two pieces of velvet right sides together and stitch around three sides. Clip the corners and turn right side out. Stuff firmly with wadding. Insert lavender or pot pourri if required. Turn under the seam allowance along the fourth side and oversew to close, leaving a small gap for inserting the ends of the braid or twisted cord trimming. Slipstitch the trimming around the edge and sew up the gap.

How to make a pencil case

Fold the velvet widthways 15cm (6in) from one

Making a pencil case, securing the turned under edges of the flap with herringbone stitch.

end and mark the fold with a line of basting stitch. Turn under a double 1cm (⅜in) hem at the top edge. Trim the aida to 1.5cm (½in) all around the edges of the design and press under, one square out from the sides and top of the design, and two squares down from the lower edge. Slipstitch the design in place 5.5cm (2¼in) down from the hemmed edge, and 5cm (2in) in from each side. Sew narrow braid or twisted cord around the edges, making a loop at each corner.

Fold the velvet right sides together along the basted line. Sew up the sides by machine or with back stitch, 1.5cm (⅝in) from the edge. Turn right side out. Turn under the raw edges of the flap and secure with herringbone stitch. Then turn under a double 1cm (⅜in) hem along the top. Sew on three buttons and make button loops to match.

How to make a covered box

Position the embroidery over the box lid, then fold the edges down over the sides and trim to fit. Remove the aida and spread glue over the top and sides of the box lid. Position the design over the lid and press in place. Pull the sides of the aida down over the lid edges and glue in place. Trim away any excess fabric at the corners. Glue a length of ribbon over the raw edges of the aida to hide them, overlapping the two ends where they meet. Turn under the uppermost ribbon end to prevent fraying. Put the lid on the box, then glue ribbon around the base so that all visible sides are covered. Glue braid around the top of the lid.

How to make a paperweight

Place the design face upon a surface and put the glass part of the paperweight on top, with the design in the centre. Draw around the edge of the paperweight. Remove the glass piece and replace with the piece of thin card, covering the design and allowing an equal border all around. Use this as a template, and draw around it. Remove the piece of card, replace it with the glass and check that the inner line fits into the inside of the paper-weight. Place the work face down into the upturned paperweight. Turn right side up, holding the design in place to make sure that it is correctly positioned. Turn it face down again and place the piece of card over the design. Finally, remove the paper from the sticky base fabric and stick it on the back of the paperweight.

How to make a large cushion

Cut the worked fabric into a circle 21cm (8¼in) in diameter, making sure that the design is positioned centrally. Press under a 1cm (⅜in) seam all around, and sew centrally onto one piece of the velvet with slipstitch, leaving a small gap. Stitch the twisted cord around the edge of the aida circle, hiding the ends in the gap. Slipstitch the gap and fasten two tassels to the base of the circle.

   Place the two pieces of velvet right sides together and sew around three sides by machine or with back stitch, taking a 1.5 cm (½ in) seam allowance. Clip the corners and turn through to the right side. Insert the cushion pad and close the fourth side with slipstitch.

How to make buttons

With the design in the centre, cut a circle of fabric 5cm (2in) in diameter for each button. Work a circle of small running stitches around the outer edge of the fabric. Place the fabric right side down and position the button head face down on the back of the design. Gather the fabric around the button. Then place the back of the button face down over the central hole and push down with a cotton reel, or follow manufacturer's instructions.

How to make a brooch

Dismantle the brooch. Position the transparent plastic oval piece over the design, ensuring that the design is centred. Draw around the oval and cut out the fabric around the line. Replace the plastic oval in the frame and place the design face down on top. Lay the brooch face down on a soft cloth and place the thin card and the velvet-backed card on top. Then, using a small coin, carefully roll the tags inward over the velvet card to keep all the layers in place.

How to make a bookmark

Using a machine zigzag stitch or oversewing by hand, stitch a line just above and below the top and bottom lines of cross stitches. Fringe the edges by pulling out the horizontal threads.

How to make a stocking

Trim the aida to 1.5cm (½in) around the outside of the design. Press under the raw edges of the fabric two squares out from the edges of the design. Cut out two stocking shapes from black velvet, measuring 00cm (00in) in height 00cm (00in) across the bottom and 00cm (00in) across the top opening. Slipstitch the embroidered panel in place 16.5cm (6½in) down from the top of one of the pieces of velvet. Pin the two pieces of velvet right sides together and stitch around the edges, leaving the top edge open. Turn under a 1cm (⅜in) hem along the top edge and stitch down. Turn right side out.

   Stitch netting or lace to the top edge of the stocking to form a decorative band. Slipstitch the ribbon around the edge of the netting to cover the raw edge, then finish with a bow.

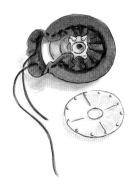

Making buttons, gathering the fabric around the button. To avoid the fabric fraying at this stage, the inner circle of running stitches should not be worked too close to the edge.

Index

Suppliers

NEEDLEWORK PRODUCTS

All DMC and Zweigart fabrics used in this book are available from DMC and Zweigart stockists throughout the world. They also supply other products, including embroidery frames, cards, needles, scissors, etc.

UK:
For details of your nearest DMC and Zweigart stockist contact:

DMC Creative World
Pullman Road
Wigston
Leicester
Leicestershire LE18 2DY

USA:
For details of your nearest DMC stockist contact:

The DMC Corporation
Port Kearny
Building 10
South Kearny
New Jersey 07032

For details of your nearest US Zweigart stockist contact:
Joan Toggitt Ltd
2 Riverview Drive
Somerset
New Jersey 08873

Australia:
For details of your nearest DMC and Zweigart stockist contact:

DMC
51-66 Carrington Road
Marrickville
New South Wales 2204

New Zealand:
For details of your nearest DMC and Zweigart stockist contact:

Warnaar Trading Co Ltd
376 Ferry Road
PO Box 19567
Christchurch

South Africa:
For details of your nearest DMC stockist contact:

SATC
43 Somerset Road
PO Box 3868
Capetown 8000

For details of your nearest Zweigart stockist contact:
Brasch Hobby
10 Loveday Street
PO Box 6405
Johannesburg 2000

ANTIQUES, LACE AND OLD POSTCARDS

Barbara Kirk
Kitts Corner
51 Chapel Street
Penzance
Cornwall
England

Janet Denise
The Dorking Antique Centre
West Street
Dorking
Surrey
England

ANTIQUE VELVET, BRAID, LACE AND TASSELS

Catherine and Mary Antiques
1 Brewery Yard
Bread Street
Penzance
Cornwall
England

PICTURE FRAMES

Pete Wayne
The Framing Studio
Bread Street
Penzance
Cornwall
England

Acknowledgements

I would like to thank my husband, Gareth, for writing the computer chart program used for all the charts in the book, and for his help and support. Also my daugher Gemma for charting the designs on the computer, and the rest of my family for putting up without complaint my working seven days a week for months on the book.

I would also like to thank Chris Kirk and Julie Harris of Readers Union and Cara Ackerman of DMC for their assistance and encouragement, Cara and Maria Diaz for supplying all the Zweigart and DMC products used in this book, Gabrielle Townsend for her enthusiasm and support, Lyn le Grice and Francine Lawrence for their faith in me, and for their help and encouragement over the years, and Catherine Ward for editing the book and Lisa Tai for designing it.

Thanks to the sewing ladies who slaved away working the designs: Catherine, Jane and Sinead Belfield; Pam Correnti; Joanne Holmes; Elaine Perkins; Tracy Robbens and Brenda Vowles.

The jetsetter desktop publishing program for this book was supplied by Jetsetter Ltd, Bread Street, Penzance, Cornwall, England.